Clare!
You are a Big
Dreamer.
Keep Going!
JqyMac

THINK

CREATE

JUMP

11 Proven Ways To Create A "Hell Yeah" Life

By Jennifer MacFarlane

**Join the conversation on my Facebook group —
AstraLily Unleash Your Brilliance**

Who This Book Is For

This book is for those who are ready to rise up! Rise up from their limited programing, Rise up from their own cycle of "I can't." If you are ready to harness your extraordinary personal power and let go of all that limits you, This book is for you! If you are ready to live your wildest dreams but feel stuck, It's you I have written for. Think Create Jump Is the message you've been seeking. Your best YOU is calling you forth, now it's up to you to... Jump!

Why I Have Written This Book

When I was younger I new I would write books, but I wouldn't say it was solely me who decided to write this book. I woke up one morning and knew it was time; the book was ready to be written. I was just lucky to be the one chosen to write it and share it with you. I sat down and my fingers didn't stop for months. It (Universe) was flowing through me. It was a time in my life when I needed to hear these messages as much you probably do now. Imagine that you have called this book to you. Now... It's your turn to discover your dreams.

Who Is Jennifer MacFarlane?

Jennifer MacFarlane (for lack of a better way to describe ("WHO I AM") Is an Bestselling Author/ Inspirational Speaker, Freedompreneur Mentor , Lifestyle Business Strategist and straight talkin' truth bomber. Jen motivates people take on their lives like "A Boss". She also plays the part of Mother, Wife, Intuitive Healer, Spiritual Guide and Visionary. Jennifer helps people from all over the world create a deeper connection with themselves and the life they want to live through her online business www.AstraLily.com

Jennifer has always had a calling to understand the connection between the mind and our reality. She has herself experienced the transformation that understanding the power of one's owns thoughts can bring and wishes to help others experience the same revelation. Jen Believes we are here to learn how to overcome our own limits and live our Biggest, Wildest Dreams.

Dream Big - Smile More (The words Jen lives by)

TABLE OF CONTENTS

INTRODUCTION

It's easy to lead an ordinary life, but it's a lot more fun to step outside of the limiting box of normality and long-established comfort zones so that the life you live is filled with extraordinary surprises. -Me

Did you ever notice that in this world we celebrate super-powerful, super-successful people: gurus, superstars, TV personalities, top chefs, bestselling authors, singers; the best of the best. The problem with "looking up" to these influential figures is that we forget to celebrate our own successes. We honor the Olympians, the star athletes, the richest people, religious leaders -- We actually worship them.

When was the last time you honored and celebrated your own value? Maybe you were never told that you were valuable. When you put somebody on a higher level than yourself, it might seem like they are empowering you, but in actuality it is dis-empowering you! As long as you are looking outside of yourself, searching outside of yourself, celebrating outside of yourself, and valuing others more than yourself you will feel worthless and you will under-value your own unique offerings in the world.

The only difference between you and popular figures like Oprah, Jesus, Buddha, Madonna, and Picasso is that they were/are living their life *on purpose.* They followed a strong charge that came from within them. That's what living on purpose feels like. They created a world where their dreams became their reality.

Imagine living a life where what you dream about and desire actually come to manifest in real time. Imagine opening your eyes every single day and being sincerely grateful that you get to wake up and do what you love! **What would that feel like?**

This book is for all the people in the world who have fallen into the trap of living for everybody else while simultaneously forgetting their own passions. This is it! This is your time to stand up and live a soul-charged life that feels good.

Live Your Dream Life

Have you ever dreamed of how freeing it would be to spend your time doing something you love? Too often we stop thinking about our own passions and desires so that we can "do our job" and take care of everybody else. Maybe you dream of becoming an iconic artist, a successful entrepreneur, a professional athlete, or even attracting a perfect lover? When I ask people the question "What do you really love to do?" I see that deep inside, under layers of limiting beliefs, we all have deep secret desires and big dreams. However, only a small percentage of people enable their dreams to become reality. So my big question was, why and what makes that small percentage of highly successful people different? Why do some people get to have it all while others struggle to get by?

Find Your True Value

How fast would your life change if you truly felt that you had purpose and value, if you believed that you had something to share with the world and that that something was valuable enough to make a difference in the lives of other people? (I'm not talking about cooking and cleaning, unless that's what lights you up inside.)

Here is a simple equation. YOU +DESIRE + PASSION = VALUE.

This equation simply means that if you are in touch with your dreams and desires and are able to reach for them with enough passion to let that part of yourself shine, if your passion can override all the naysayers, all the negative people who will try to stop you, if your passion can fuel your life, then and only then will you understand your own power. When you simply can't shut down the passion that fuels your soul, then you will understand your value.

What does being passionate about something feel like?
Many of you have forgotten. In this book you're going to come to understand your value, dig up your hidden talents and unique gifts, your wisdom and knowledge, your deepest secrets and unused skills and use them to create a life that is charged with passion.

Through this book you will free up parts of your soul that you've forgotten even existed. You will cut through layers and layers and more layers of yourself that you have totally forgotten about. It's time to light up our souls!

I want to empower as many people as possible to love being alive. After all, a person charged with Happiness is one of the strongest forces in the Universe, but that powerful energy has been dumbed down, scattered and not taken seriously. Unfortunately, the opposite is also true: a person who is angry, depressed, overwhelmed and sad is also a powerful force. I hope that we will all learn the power of being a creator, the power of giving birth to the new. This is the power you harness. Unleash it!

This book is for the powerful people who no longer want their dreams simply taking up space in their heads and are ready to take action and make their dreams a reality. This is your time! Time to live with the surging fire of passion in your belly. It's time to show the world who you are! And for your dreams to burst with vitality!

The 11 chapters in this book will bring clarity on who you are at the deepest level. I strongly believe that we all have big dreams, burning desires and passions that ache to be realized. When we acknowledge these feelings everything comes alive inside of us and then and only then will we be able to understand the value that we have to offer to the world. Nobody else can give you or show you this high value you acquire. You must find your value, feel your value and believe it yourself. You simply cannot depend on the feeling that others bring when they value you because they can't truly value you until you value yourself. When you start to see and believe in the value of your unique gifts, your hidden talents, your desires, your wisdom, your knowledge, your secret dreams, and you start to see how this value could serve others, you will experience:

- **Your extraordinary power**
- **Great freedom**
- **More happiness and joy**
- **The joy of appreciating your value in the world**
- **A charge of universal flow because of your ability to listen to your intuition**
- **The opportunity to create more money doing what you love**
- **Great confidence**
- **Less pain and disease in the body**
- **More energy and vitality from releasing emotional blocks**
- **Ease and flow - Things will line up and fall into place for you**
- **Yourself as a creator**
- **Sleep better because your mind is calmer**
- **Unbelievable synchronicities**

So, What's Stopping You?

I know all of this making your dreams come true stuff sounds good, but, how do you move past your roadblocks? Well, first you have to understand why you constantly become stopped and become aware of the excuses that you use over and over again. Just being aware of these things is *gold* in overcoming our limited actions. Notice the same things that come up for you especially when you get close to the end of a specific goal.

Maybe you get sick, or a certain disease in your body starts to act up. I have one friend who always subconsciously comes down with a debilitating form of vertigo just before she accomplishes a big goal. This is her body's subconscious way of holding her back.

One of the biggest roadblocks I hear from people is "I'm just too tired." Being tired is a sign that your body is trying to check out! It's literally trying to shut down. So why would you do that? Because you have become very comfortable with the life you have. The thing is… These roadblocks feel real and until you know how to overcome them, they will stop you repeatedly in every area of your life. You convince yourself that you can't move forward because you believe your own fears and limiting beliefs are true.

Here is a list of excuses that become habitual roadblocks that keep people from accomplishing their dreams. Do any of them resonate with you?

- **There isn't enough money - I'm broke.**
- **I don't have any support.**
- **I'm too old.**
- **I don't have enough energy.**
- **My body isn't healthy enough.**
- **I'm just too tired.**
- **I'm sick / limited by my body or disease.**
- **It's too hard.**
- **I don't know how to do it.**
- **My family wouldn't understand.**
- **I don't have enough education.**
- **I've tried before and failed.**
- **There simply isn't enough time.**
- **I have to take care of my family first/ what would my family think.**
- **It costs too much.**

Have you said any of these things to yourself (or out loud) in the past? If so, Get ready to stop using such deflating mental language and get ready to start saying "Hell Yeah" to your dreams and desires.

I know it's easy to do, to live a life of excuses instead of saying "Yes" and going for it. I have participated in all of the habitual roadblocks above myself and my experience is that you never really know when one of these limiting excuses is going to sneak in, take over your life and stop you! Once you become aware of your own programmed limitations and stop giving them power, you will surprise yourself at what you will feel on the other side of the roadblock: *freedom!* You will always try to stop yourself when you are close to a *"big something."*

If you become a master at charging through your limitations with passion, you will experience *huge breakthroughs!* You will surprise yourself and you will start to realize that it was never the sickness or the fatigue or the lack of money that got in the way of your success, it was you! **The roadblock is just a manifestation of how you are presently programmed.** As long as you are unaware of these roadblocks, you will keep doing what you have been doing and ending up where you have always ended up.

I Was Programmed To Lose, But Now I Live My "Hell Yeah" Life!

I didn't always feel purposeful, nor did I believe I had any value in the world. In fact, I spent the first twenty-five years of my life feeling that I had no value at all. I grew up in a small town In Nova Scotia on a road called Black Hole Road. As you can imagine, Black Hole Road was not the most inspiring place to grow up. I grew up in a pretty dysfunctional home, My Father drank a lot. He would come out of nowhere, angry, red-eyed, sloppy, unkind, loud and annoying.

One time, for instance, I was just hanging out listening to music in my bedroom when I heard the stairs creaking, I knew my drunken father was coming and I didn't want to see him. I locked my door and he banged on it loudly, yelling "Let me in" in his drunken voice, He eventually busted the door open and I was so scared and hated him so much right in that moment that I hid under my desk!

I feared him intensely, and although he was never physically abusive his face carried such frantic anger that as a young girl it terrified me. For years I begged my mother to divorce him.

One time I wanted him out of the house so much that I even packed all of his clothes into black garbage bags, put an Alcohol Anonymous book on top of them and left them outside the front door.

Eventually, my mother took us to family counseling and I looked my father in the face and said, "I hate you." He looked back at me straight in the eyes and said, "I hate you too."

I remember the heart-wrenching pain I felt, I was broken.

I was alone, and I hated myself.

I started stealing prescription pills from my Mom's dresser drawers and medicine cabinets at friends' houses. I had a couple of bottles of pills that I'd collected, and one day, when I had had enough, I grabbed my bottles of mixed prescription drugs, swallowed them all as fast as I could. As insurance I even went to the basement where I found a bottle of tree poison. I washed the collection of mixed drugs down with a few big gulps of this thick black liquid, wrote my Mom a goodbye letter, and fell asleep. All I remember is my Mother screaming "Wake up! Wake up!" and I woke up puking in the hospital. I was mad that I was still alive. I was so ready to die.

Even this experience didn't turn my life around. Things didn't get better for a long time. As I moved into my teen years, I hated school and sucked at it! All of my friends smoked, did drugs and drank, my boyfriends slept around, dealt drugs and de-valued me. I struggled to wake up in the mornings, I had no drive, watched as other girls received athletic trophies, become honor students and held hands with the boyfriends I knew I could never get. I hated myself and my life. None of it felt fair.

Nobody ever told me I had potential. I never heard the words "Good Job." In fact, people made fun of me throughout most of my adolescence. I never dreamed because nobody ever told me I could. My sister and I didn't get swimming lessons or dance lessons; there wasn't money for us to do anything extra. We never even talked about extra-curricular activities because we didn't know they existed.

I didn't grow up knowing anybody successful. Everybody in our town was the same. Everybody struggled.

Nobody had opportunity, and everybody was angry and unhappy. The divorce rate amongst my friends' parents was 99%. When it came to graduation time (which I can't believe actually happened) I was told by my Mother that a student loan was not an option for me because of her limited income and the recent divorce of her and my father. So I didn't even look into higher education. At this point and up until I was twenty-two years old, my blueprint was meek. I had no ambition because I was programmed to believe that there wasn't anything more then what I had experienced in my life thus far. I didn't know it could be different **because I didn't know anything different.** I had been programmed to fail.

How I overcame my Limited Mind and started to create an Unlimited Life

I was nineteen years old when my best friend Michelle called me and said, "Lets pack up and find jobs in Banff." At the time I didn't even know where Banff was! The world that I was aware of was smaller than you can imagine. At this time, I was so ready for change that I jumped at the opportunity and after a couple of telephone interviews we both had jobs and were ready to go.

Neither one of us had even driven on a highway, but we packed Michelle's little car to the roof with all of our belongings, I kissed my Mother goodbye and we drove across the country from Nova Scotia to Alberta. I felt *free* for the first time!

This was the beginning of a new life for me. I just knew things would be different. The truth is… Things were different.

Banff is a beautiful town, lots of change, people with accents, opportunities. But… I hadn't changed - I was numb. I still had so much pain that I couldn't deal with and I fell into the party scene for many years. Thank goodness, all was not wasted as this is when I met my dream boy who is now my wonderful husband.

For the first time in my life I had met a guy who showed me real love, I owe my life to this man. He made me feel like a princess (and still does.) He wrote me love letters and brought me flowers, he showed me that I deserved to be loved, that I was beautiful and with the bounty of his love my confidence slowly started to rise.

As my vibration started to rise, people started coming into my life that offered value and were interested in my success. One day when I was working at the Greyhound bus station, a lady from accounting challenged me. "I see you reading all these books on Alternative Health and Yoga, so why on earth are you working at a bus station?"

I didn't really know what to say, but in that moment I realized that I was wasting my time sitting in a dimly lit room selling tickets to people and shipping parcels. "Would you be interested in coming to a workshop I'm hosting this Wednesday?" she said. "It's about removing blockages from the past so that you can move passionately into the future." I was intrigued – and nervous, but little did I know that this conversation would change my life forever.

She looked at me and said something I will never forget. "I take a stand for people's greatness, and I see your greatness." As she walked away I felt as though my throat had been sucker-punched. I couldn't speak, My heartbeat sped up, and I had never felt so strange before, I wanted to cry but I didn't, I couldn't.

Before this moment I had no idea that I had any greatness to stand for.

Up until that moment all my teachers, coaches, friends, and family had only pointed out what I wasn't good at, so my deeply ingrained belief was that I had no value. But that was all about to change. I went to a one-hour life-changing personal development course and signed up right there and then for their three-day workshop.

That three-day workshop immediately *changed my life*.

After I finished the three-day program my fears slowly started to disappear and I started creating a more fulfilling life. I realized that I loved yoga and Pilates, so I moved to Toronto for four months to do my Stott Pilates Teacher training and immerse myself in Yoga. When I finished my training I opened my own business called OM PILATES. My business was very successful and I started to understand my value. A year and a half later, I became pregnant. During my pregnancy I developed a debilitating form of sciatica and couldn't walk for four months. I had no choice but to close my business and sell all of my equipment. This was another heartbreaking time in my life. I was like "SERIOUSLY!!!!"

Because of my sciatica I could never return to the Pilates world so I turned to yoga. I did yoga every day and acquired a love for myself through it. I went on retreats, visited Ashrams and started reading everything I could about Yoga. Yoga became a part of me and I became the Yoga. It allowed me to journey into the deepest layers of myself. The next logical step was to find a Yoga teacher training. I was particularly interested in Kundalini Yoga. Funny as it is, when I started searching, I found out that there was a teacher-training course starting in a few months in the next town over from where I was living. I promptly registered for the course and eagerly waited for it to start.

This was the first time I started to believe that the Universe had a plan for me because things started falling into place faster and easier than I could have ever imagined. After years of practice and teaching and leading workshops, I added Yin Yoga training and Restorative Yoga training to my body of knowledge. This book is a compilation of the most powerful life changing tools that have been passed down along the way of my own success. It is a roadmap for how to overcome all the no's, all the blockages, and your own limited programming.

You have become afraid of your greatness -- both of achieving it and of failing to achieve it -- but your dream is what makes you great; it is your gift to share with the world. Believe in yourself beyond your circumstance, beyond what you've been told and beyond your own limiting thoughts and opinions.

Because somebody once stood for my greatness, I can now stand for yours. I am clear that we are all great, that we all have something of extraordinary value to offer, that our own unique gifts and hidden talents can make a huge difference in the world. But most importantly, we can begin to love ourselves again.

You Are Powerful and Smart and Brilliant

Begin to listen to the wisdom inside yourself. What you hear is not only a message for yourself, but also a message that wants to be shared from the Universe with the rest of the world through you. Each one of you has this power. This book is a collaboration of inspirations to help *you* find and live your purpose. When you are living your purpose, all things become available to you.

As I was writing this book, I experienced something quite profound; I realized that, though I thought I was writing for the reader, I needed to hear these words myself. I was deepening my own understanding of these techniques and deepening my own sense of value and purpose. Someone with a Ph.D. didn't write the words that you read here; I'm not a scientist, nor a highly religious person. In my physical form I am an average person. I have a nine-year-old son. I teach yoga. I am married and I have waitressed for many years. I would venture a guess that I experience the same emotional ups and downs as you, and I've always had big dreams. Recently, something has changed for me. I've had an awakening, a call to action -- an inner knowing -- that has shown me that *now* is the time to make these dreams happen, and I am being led to empower others to do the same.

For the past 15 years I have immersed myself in different spiritual practices and the right teachers have always come into my life at the right time. I asked for guidance and the Universe responded with speed. The words you are about to read are not only mine; to look at me, you certainly wouldn't think to yourself, "What an enlightened being!" I have been given a chance to show you that we are all enlightened. I want to show you that whether you're Buddha or a drunk on the street, you have incredible power and you are powerfully valuable. You have inside you the wisdom, the love, and the ability to share your purpose and gifts, knowledge and experiences with the world. I want to empower you to use who you are to live fully, with a charged soul, to create anything that you desire. Make some magic happen!

Always remember that you have something valuable to offer. You are here at this time for a reason that you don't yet understand. Powerful friend; I ask you, what is your dream? Let's spend this time together building our worlds and dreaming together. Let's wake up the dormant dimensions of your imagination. Only you possess the thoughts, desires, and unique touch that will create anew this world in which we live. Maybe you want to share your music with the world, or travel and share a piece of yourself with the other inhabitants of this incredible planet. Maybe you love food and are able to demonstrate that love to others. The real question you must ask yourself is, do you have the courage to share what you love with the rest of the world? And are you ready to do that with great enthusiasm? Your golden ticket in life is your gift! Find it. Share it proudly and let the world know who you are!

Universe's Insight:

"Powerful People, when you hold your dream in your thoughts, nurture it with repetition and start following the intuitive path that the Universe places in front of you and enthusiastically take action, you will notice that not only do your dreams come true, but you get much more than you could have ever imagined. There is more that has been laid out for you then you are able to perceive. You often see only one dimension of our dream at a time."

In essence, it's up to you to feel happy; consider it your divine right to be a shining light of ultimate happiness. You were born a being. That's right; start acting like you *deserve* to be incredibly happy! If you're ready for it, if you're ready to be and have everything you've ever imagined and beyond, then come on this journey and realize your gifts. Realize your purpose and start doing what you are here to do.

Journey with me to a place of infinite possibility, to a place beyond what you think and believe to be true.

If you're stuck, take the first step.

You have a secret desire burning inside of you, so spark the flame and let it roar. I believe in you! Trust me, I know you have been waiting a long time to realize and use your gift. And I know it can be terrifying at times, but this is it: your golden ticket to living the life you've dreamed of. You can crawl, walk, or run; it doesn't matter how fast you move toward your dreams, because they are moving towards you at the same speed. It will happen because you hold within you the spark of that desire, a spark that will never ever leave you. It may fall asleep and move into your subconscious, but it will always be there waiting for you to rekindle it.

CHAPTER 1 THE POWER OF YOUR BREATH

THE MOST POWERFUL THING THEY NEVER TAUGHT YOU IN SCHOOL

Universe's Insight: "Breath is the vehicle for life force and universal energy to enter your body, carrying with it an essential vitality. Isn't that what you really want: to feel alive, happy, and energized? Your breath is what connects you—your physical form—to all that is; it gives your body life. Within the breath is the energy of everything that has ever been, everything that is and everything that will ever be. Your breath has been gifted to you as a means of connecting to the Universe, the source of all energy. You must first understand that everything is energy. With each breath you are bringing life into you; it's a natural process given to you when you enter this world as you know it now."

Unfortunately, it's easy for people to get wound up in everything that is happening around them outside their physical body. The people, the news, the economy, world issues, natural disasters, envy of others, grocery lists, to-do lists, exercise programs, judging what's good and bad, cleaning our homes, paying bills, appointments, kids, pets, work…. You've forgotten about the most important thing: *you!* Your breath has the sweet power to bring you back to the calm, quiet place that resides deep inside you. You could be in the middle of the busiest train station in Tokyo, or witnessing a bank robbery, or in an argument with your spouse; however, if you are connected to your breath, you will have the ability to stay calm in any situation. Breathing is always there, it's always with you; you don't have to pack it, you just have to remember that it's there when you need it.

When you feel anxious, frustrated, angry, or any other uncomfortable emotion, you'll notice that your breath becomes very shallow. It often feels as if your power has been completely taken away, as if your mind has become a torturous place where you are unable to order your thoughts.

Become conscious of how you breathe. Become one with your source. If you teach yourself to take long, deep breaths throughout the day, you will automatically use your breath to your advantage when difficult situations arise. In doing so, you'll be able to ride the waves of unpredictability on the ocean of life instead of resisting, judging what's happening, and ending up crashing up against the rocks.

Simply take a deep breath through your nose. Fill your belly, ribs, and chest all the way up to your collar bone and then open your mouth and let the exhalation explode out of your mouth with the intention of deep letting go. Take as many of these breaths as you need until those uncomfortable emotions -- those feelings of anxiety, fear, pain, and anger -- subside. When you do this, it is like you are hitting a reset button. It's so simple – and, like I mentioned before, it's always with you! By using your breath in a conscious way, you literally increase your power.

I feel compelled to share with you the wisdom of Thich Nhat Hanh. "Breath is the bridge which connects life to consciousness, which unites your body to your thoughts. Whenever your mind becomes scattered, use your breath as a means to take hold of your mind again." I love how in such few words Thich Nhat Hanh manages to express this message so clearly.

Observe your breathing right now, without trying to control it in any way. How does it feel, what sounds are associated with it, what parts of your body move when you breathe? Does it feel stuck or blocked anywhere? Feel its natural rhythm. Often when we slow the breath down, we start to hear the crazy chatter of our crazy minds. Breathe and listen. Breathe and listen. This is how you will come to understand the question "Who am I?" You will see that you as well as how you view the world are a manifestation of your own thoughts, and the stories that you tell yourself.

Life Enhancing Breathing Technique #1

Easy Breathe

I mentioned this technique earlier in the chapter.

Inhale long and deep, fill your belly, ribcage and chest; all the way up to your collar bone. Exhale, let the breath explode out of your mouth as if you're trying to fog up a window with your breath.

Give it a try. Feel the deep release. Do this for as long as you need to or until you feel a state of peace return to your *mind and body.*

I learned about the powerful effects of breathing when I took my first yoga class. Breathing at the time was not the reason I had begun my yogic journey. I hadn't even thought about my breath at that time except when recognizing how much breath I didn't have when I ran. Ujjayi Breath (a breathing technique commonly used in the power yoga world) was very difficult for me and I honestly didn't see the point. It felt like a waste of time for me! I was there for two reasons: balance in my life and get ripped. It simply seemed to be the best way to get the body I'd dreamed of.

At the time, Madonna was showing up in the media as the superstar who became ripped doing yoga. And I thought perhaps it would complement my breathless running program. After many years of doing different styles of yoga I ended up at some classes that were very different from the typical power/Vinyassa yoga I had been doing. I took a restorative yoga class where I felt the breath in my body for the first time.

It amazed me that I had been breathing my whole life and even controlling it in my yoga practice but had never in a relaxed way experienced the feeling of the breath moving in and out of my body, expanding as I inhaled, contracting as I exhaled. Shortly after this experience I ended up with a book in my lap about breathing techniques and lo and behold when I lay in my bed at night practicing only breathing techniques I found myself! Thank God I didn't have to travel around the world to find me; there I was in the raw! I felt renewed, and it was so simple! I understood the force of life that traveled through my body via the breath when I inhaled.

This experience was far more intricate a discovery than just merely breathing in oxygen. I could heal through the breath, I could become calm in one breath and to be able to stop anger and frustration in its track was truly a magical life-enhancing thing. Although I confess that I still forget to consciously breathe sometimes when I could really benefit from its power. I know I will only continue to get better and better every day.

Universe's Insight: "The first thing that you do when you enter this world is take a big breath. This first breath signifies the beginning of this life; you bring life force into you, typically followed by a huge scream! This is understandable, considering you're leaving the warm, comfortable, safe, and connected spiritual realm of your mother's belly. Life happens, years pass, you laugh, you cry, you go crazy a few times, and then you die. And what signifies your last moment of this life is when you take your last breath. If you think about this, what you will come to realize is that there is the beginning

(inhalation) and the end (exhalation) and everything else in between is life. This leads you to explore the question, what is this life that the breath brings into us?"

In the Yogic texts it is called Prana. In ancient Chinese medicine they call it Chi. Japanese martial arts identify it as Ki or Qi. It has been referred to as the life force and as Universal energy. What happens between the first and last breath -- between life and death -- is a series of energy flows that map your path.

When did you stop breathing? That's a ridiculous question, isn't it? Of course you haven't stopped breathing! The breath is controlled by the autonomic nervous system, the part of the brain that controls the beating of the heart, respiration, perspiration, salivation, sexual arousal, and so much more. The autonomic nervous system is always at work just below your level of consciousness. This is a very good thing, because if you had to think about how to make sure that all of these things were done properly every second, you wouldn't have time for anything else at all. How would we ever be able to go to sleep? Your body is such an amazing gift, a whole Universe at work within you. This is how nature works, and this is where the magic starts!

Have you ever watched a baby breathe? A baby has not yet let the stress of life shorten and limit their breath. The belly of a baby fills like a balloon and takes in the energy and force of life that it needs to thrive. As we grow many different things cause us to lose our life-giving breath. As a woman who was quite depressed as a teenager I passed through stages of eating disorders and suicidal tendencies and low self-confidence. I could swear I didn't breathe at all through these years; I was so disconnected from my source, my own spirit. Out of all the psychiatric help I received I think that re-learning how to breathe would have helped me tremendously.

If I could teach the people of the world one thing it would be power breathing. It's the best medicine. It brings you out of the craziness and back to the essence of you. Most people are depriving themselves of breath (life force), for many reasons, some subconscious. People are completely unaware of the thoughts they are having over and over again like a broken record, like - you're not good enough, your fat, suck it in, pull your belly in, you're a failure, you can't do it, And some are consciously chosen thoughts like my belly is fat, I want to lose 10 pounds, I totally failed or I can't do it. Both subconscious and conscious thoughts cause us to tense up and constrict the breath.

I remember watching my sister get dressed for school when very tight jeans were in style. She would lie on her bed and pull her zipper up with a clothes hanger! I'm sure she didn't breathe fully for many years. (I Love You Sis!)

Some people wear clothes that actually impede their ability to breathe deeply. Some people eat so much in one sitting that the diaphragm doesn't have enough room to breathe full deep breaths. Most people who smoke become addicted to the feeling of the deep inhalation and long exhalation. If you are a smoker, when are you the most likely to get the need pulling at you to go for a smoke? More often than not it would be when you got into a heated discussion where your breathing became shallow, when you worked so hard that you couldn't take a deep breath. Life becomes so busy that we just forget about the breath, so luckily the body remembers to breathe itself.

Take a moment to close your eyes and listen to your breath, listen to the sound of your breath moving through your nostrils, through the nasal passage, the back of your throat. Feel your breath as a welcome universal force entering the body, filling the belly, back, ribs, chest and heart. Hear the sounds of the breath, notice if one nostril is more open the other. Spend a few intimate moments with your breath, focus 100% of your attention and energy. Let your breath tell you a story; listen long enough for the story to be heard. One fully focused breath can change your whole perspective. One full deep breath can bring you peace. One full intimate breath can bring you back to you when the shit has hit the fan and everything around has fallen out of balance. On a positive note, the breath deepens our experience with source. It sweetens the Experience of life!

It is amazing to think that just one moment, one breath can make you new. So it is no surprise that the breath is the first gift we are given when we exit the womb and enter this world. It is the magic tool that you always have with you.

People pay a lot of money for prescriptions that give this sense of balance, that inner state of peace, but you know the Universe really did give us everything we need to thrive here. The breath is no mistake. We are our breath. You'll notice people that breathe very shallow seem to be angry, unbalanced and even crazy. While people who breathe long deep breaths seem to be calm, you enjoy being around them; their energy is good, peaceful, happy and uplifting.

You're only a breath away from being fulfilled and happy right now in your life. Doesn't it sound a little too good to be true, like a magic pill? Let me tell you, if I could bottle full deep breaths and sell them as a miracle drug I'd be a very rich person. You would be happy to pay for it! We all would! What we all want is to feel good, to be balanced and healthy, and to allow the mystery of life to be an unfolding, to fully accept and love ourselves and share that state of bliss with those around us! Yes, this is what we are after on some level or another. This is the great gift you were given to connect to yourself, I think that the Universe knew that shit was going to get crazy and sent us here with the proper tools to not only get by, but to thrive! You are meant to thrive here - *now!*

Life Enhancing Breathing Technique # 2: The Five-Count Breath

Done through the nose

Inhale now, a long, slow, and deep breath. Exhale slowly. Count to five as you inhale, pausing at the top of this inhalation for a count of one, and then slowly exhale as you count to five, pausing at the bottom for another count of one. Keep going with this breath—inhale, count to five, pause for one, exhale for five, and pause for one. Close your eyes and count out five more of these full, deep breaths. Seriously, put this book down and continue with five more deep breaths, inhaling for 1, 2, 3, 4, 5, pause 1, and exhale 5, 4, 3, 2, 1, pause again for 1. You're not even reading this right now because you have already put the book down, right? If you haven't, stop reading now and put the book down. Breathe! I'll meet you back here in a couple minutes.

(Five long life-enhancing deep breaths later...)

Ok, welcome back! Do you feel like a different person now? Did you feel a shift within you? Your body loves deep breaths. Your mind finds balance as its busy chatter slows down so you can actually hear your thoughts. Your body feels energized. I often feel tingling sensations in my body after just a few deep breaths.

So, what is the science behind the breath?

I love science but, I am not a scientist so when I research a subject, I arrange the information in a way that makes sense to me (don't we all.) You'll soon see that the way that I think is how I see the world. I love that the first thing I read when looking for the science of the breath is that *inhalation* is also referred to as *inspiration,* and *exhalation* is referred to as *expiration.* In essence, what you have is a continuous flow of life and death. The science of power breathing supports the need of oxygen to the body so that it has energy, which I'm sure is very important; however, I think I've got what I came here for with the inspiration and expiration thing. Breathe it into you; let it go. Breathe it into you; let it go. Breathe it into you; let it go.

It is the cycle of life happening within us with every breath.

The Universe is delighted as I toss this idea around in my head and sends a clear message to the front of my mind; the message is: opportunity.

Universe's Insight: "Every breath is an opportunity for something new. If you want something, breathe it into you, and make each breath a dedicated moment where you visualize what you want entering you on the inspiration (inhalation) and let it go on the expiration (exhalation). This letting go represents your non-attachment to the outcome while the ebb and flow of inspiration and expiration represent the natural cycle of life and death."

Life Enhancing Breathing Technique #3: Inspiration and Expiration

Inhale deeply, visualize an inspiring idea, exhale and let it go. Imagine that all things travel through the life force of the breath. You can pull them into you like a vacuum and you can let them go.

Repeat. Inhale/Inspiration - Exhale/ Let It Go

Continue until you feel the excitement of your inspirations coming alive inside of you.

Lift yourself up first!

You can lift the whole world up only when you have lifted yourself up first. There is a reason why they tell you to put your own oxygen mask on before assisting others on an airplane. If you don't assist yourself first, then you are not going to be able to help anybody else.

You can put this scenario into action with any situation in life. If you have no money, you cannot give people in need money. If you don't lift yourself up first, you will not be able to lift anybody else up. If you don't love yourself, you can't give love. If you can't see the greatness in yourself, you can't help others realize their greatness. You get the point: when you become clear and when you are living for you, it will be natural for you to be a catalyst for others to realize and manifest their lives in a joyful way.

It's not about what you do; it's about the vibration of who you are. People will want to be around you, they will pay just to be in the same room as you, they will anxiously await your next book, your next song, your next goal, dance your next dance, speak your next word, or take your next breath -- not because of what you do, but because they feel good when they are around your energy.

People pay hundreds, even thousands of dollars, to see their favorite singers, Athletes, speakers, or inspirational figures like the Dali Lama, but not solely because of what they do. One can go watch any old band playing in a pub, go to a university lecture, or go to church for free; you see, it's not what these people are doing, but rather who they are that attracts crowds to them.

It's your *energy* that either attracts people to you or repels them away from you. This energy is brought to you via the breath channel.

Here is the trick: live your most authentic you. Share what you love, live what you love, and be that. Walk the walk, talk the talk, and hold the thoughts in your mind that support what you love. Nurture this part of yourself by watching people that inspire you, and practice listening to the vibration that elevates you. But most importantly... *Breathe* this power into you.

Universe's Insight: When you are nurturing your gift, it grows like a garden, multifaceted and strong. Your attention to it is like water and sun, the food that helps it

grow. Before you know it, the time has come to harvest the fruit. Your garden is just waiting to bloom. In the beginning, you need not see what will come; you just need to plant the seed. Feed it and it will feed you! Great things will come to you.

"Remember - Breathe it into you!"

CHAPTER 2 INTUITIVE LISTENING

UNDERSTAND AND USE THE GUIDANCE OF YOUR INNER TEACHER

The Universe's Insight -

"Take time to listen to your thoughts. After all, you are your thoughts. When you take time daily to listen, you begin to understand who you are, how you have manifested what you have and why you feel the way you feel. Sit with this insight and listen to what comes up for you. Mentally repeat, I am the creator of my life. I am creating my life with my thoughts in each new moment."

What a beautiful morning. I woke up before the sun to practice yoga in the quiet, Peaceful energy of the ambrosial morning something I highly recommend! Then I curled up into fetal position in bed with my son Noah. The warmth and Love traveled through every internal stream and every synapse and within all the billions of cells that make up this human being. I can feel the energy of my heart opening and growing.

After a scrumptious breakfast we went out for our morning adventure with our dog Harvey. We took a trail that we take often, except it felt entirely different, magical, like it, "Nature," was breathing us, it all felt so surreal.

I made an effort to take time to be fully in the experience of being alive in this moment. I leaned up against a tree, which had been growing on a diagonal and closed my eyes to meditate on the sounds and smells and feel the energy from the tree I lay upon.

I felt its roots and strength throughout the entire forest and then visualized it spreading its roots to expand through the Earth. I felt the deep connection that we are one huge microcosm in all microcosms. I felt gratitude for the tree, for its taking in of our waste products and giving back pure oxygen to breathe.

I heard Noah chanting Ong Namo Guru Dev Namo, a chant for evoking the divine inner wisdom within. I opened my eyes to see what he was doing: he had found himself a tree trunk that had been raised about 5 feet in the air from other trees in a pile, he was sitting in a simple cross-legged posture with his eyes closed. It looked like he was levitating.

I wished I had brought my camera or a video recording device. I hadn't, so I took a picture in my mind. We wandered around the forest sitting in different places, looking at moss and the extension of the tree roots, breathing the fresh, clean, almost hypnotic, magical air, totally taking our time. These days are so sacred. Right now I am grateful for being alive and being surrounded by such extraordinary love.

We started with the Breath in Chapter One because the breath gives you access to observe your thoughts. Try to develop a regular routine of taking twenty long, deep breaths. When you are fully connected to your breath and listening to your thoughts, you connect to who you are. What you are is a concoction of your thoughts.

Let the breath be your vehicle to great listening. You will see that your listening skills become stronger and more focused as you practice. You will start to hear your thoughts more clearly. You may get great insights during this time of listening; your anger and fears, dreams and desires will become loud enough that you can finally hear what is being asked of you. Do you believe that you are here on this planet at this time for a reason? Do you feel you have a purpose? It is your birthright to be happy, to find joy, and to feel fulfilled by what you are doing.

You might want to ask yourself, what are my thoughts creating?

I believe that the energy of our thoughts is extremely powerful and that our thoughts do create our reality. I have experienced this theory at work in my own life. When I am feeling happy and filled with joy and am focused on abundance, allowing time for the creative force of daydreaming as part of my daily practice, I experience the world around me as a party, a dance, and more money flows into my life. I feel taken care of and my vibration is higher. When I am focused on what I don't want in my life, the lack of finances, what I don't want in my relationship, how much I dislike my job, and how horrible the world is, the world and the way I see and experience it changes drastically.

For years I have felt the contrast of feeling good and feeling bad move from one to the other leaving me with ultimate highs and ultimate lows. I guess in some professions I may have been diagnosed with bi-polar disorder and depression at times, and then at the same time people sometimes ask, what do you do to be so positive? Have you always been so happy?

When the movie about the law of attraction -- *The Secret* -- came out in 2006, I started paying attention to my thoughts and how I was creating my life. Once I started listening, really listening, I understood why I had the life I had, because it was all being created by my thoughts! When I focused my energy on scarcity, that's what appeared. I never thought about how beautiful I was. My thoughts were more directed on things like not being as pretty as others and having small breasts. I focused on what my imperfections were and knew that I would never fit in with the pretty sexy girls. As a result I struggled with eating disorders and depression as a teenager.

When I came to understand the power that my thoughts had on the unfolding of my life I started making a conscious effort to say loving things to myself daily. And it was like lifting the blinders, the world as I had been experiencing it looked and felt different. I saw beauty, I felt beautiful, and I noticed the beauty of nature and felt more stable. Our thoughts are a powerful force that we do have a certain amount of control over, when we spend time listening to our subconscious thoughts we can start to choose more helpful ones, rather than letting the thoughts that you don't want run the show you can choose thoughts and start co-creating your life and how you see, believe and experience it.

You can guide those thoughts and paint the picture of how you see, believe, and experience life.

Universe's Insight:

"You are very wise.

You are not just a physical body -- legs, eyes, brain heart, and hands.

You are infinite wisdom, infinite joy, and infinite love.

Let yourself experience this."

WATCH YOUR THOUGHTS LIKE A HAWK

Donna, a beautiful and wise friend of mine gave me this simple and powerful tool years ago: "Watch yourself like a *hawk*." When she said this I had the vision of a *hawk* circling around the top of my head as if it were hunting for food, yet the *hawk* was wise and peaceful. I started to put this vision to work as a tool for listening to my thoughts. And it works like a charm.

The *hawk* is the observer of thought, thoughts running at light speed through the mind, often the same thoughts over and over again like a broken record. And when the *hawk* sees a thought that is not in alignment with what you are wanting it brings attention to it, lifts it up so you can have a really good look at what your creating in that moment. And as thoughts seem to circulate themselves repeatedly you might question how long this thought has been there conspiring with the universe to bring that to you, you become aware of this thought with the wise eyes of the *hawk* of your inner truth.

Imagine if you became aware of what your thoughts have been saying, you're ugly; nobody will ever love you, what a failure, for 25 years. You have been tricked into believing this, you have been thought- washed, this silent thought has been creating you, conspiring with the universe to make you fat and ugly and unloved because the universe hears all thought as an opportunity to create and has given to you that which you have focused on!

You realize that you never had a chance against these lies, you feel manipulated, saddened that you allowed this silent verbal attack and self-diminishing thought cycle to go on for so long.

Now that your inner hawk has pointed out this thought to you, acknowledge it, be grateful that now you know, there is awareness, now you can start to recreate yourself from this listening. Choose the thought that you would like to create! I am beautiful, perfect and am surrounded by beauty. Replace the thoughts that you no longer want to create your life with, the ones your inner *hawk* is bringing to your attention. You will start to see results quickly.

One thing to be aware of with this tool is to make sure that your thoughts are not being replaced with thoughts like, I don't want to be… or, no more... The Universe still hears your plea and brings more of this to you because this is what you are focused on! As time goes on you may start to see how crazy you are, how what you want and what you are thinking are not aligned, therefore bringing results that you don't want! Believe that you are the creator of your life, the thoughts that you have are the way that you communicate and make things happen in the universe. It's not like magic. It *is* magic.

THE THOUGHT VORTEX - You're bigger than you think

Imagine that you have a big invisible energy field that surrounds your whole body and it extends seven feet out in all directions. All of the thoughts that you've ever had are floating around in this vortex.

All of your dreams, wishes, all of your judgments, what you believe to be true, your self-imposed limitations, who you love, dislike, rights and wrongs, feelings and emotions are all in this vortex.

You will come to realize that you have really been thinking the same thoughts over and over and over again. You are *Crazy* if you do the same thing over and over again and expect different results. So I think it's safe to say at this point that we are all to some extent insane.

How can you be having the same thoughts that you have had for most of your life, like I'm a failure, I don't deserve it, I'm ugly, fat, stupid, nobody cares, not good enough and expect to be successful at anything? Your thoughts have literally told you this over and over and over again and now you believe it! You have actually become these things.

The first thing you must change is the way you think. Replace your thoughts, choose thoughts that start to empower you as the person you really want to be, think and feel successful, beautiful and sexy. When you believe it, you'll see it and others will too!

When you can see where you are limited, simply by listening to your thoughts you can acknowledge these limitations, jump over them and begin your journey as a limitless being. We must start to realize that all of our limitations exist in our minds. Once you begin the journey of going beyond your self-imposed limitations your life will flow with unlimited abundance. You'll see the world as an offering to you.

Once you realize that on a subconscious level you have been pushing the things that you want away from you, you can then start to pull in to you what you do want. Enjoy the unfolding and the contrast. Enjoy the great uncovering of limiting thoughts.

Find comfort in knowing from your deepest source of wisdom that we are all struggling with the same limited ways of being. Begin to listen to all the little messages, all calls to action and all the thoughts and inspirations. Notice the signs!

When we can see beyond these subconscious, always-happening, limiting thoughts, we are connecting to the flow of consciousness that moves through us. When you hear a message from the Universe for the first time, you will experience one of those aha moments!! As you feel like you're being pointed in a clear direction.

There is a shift that happens as you start to understand your unlimited self, your *infinite* self, the part of you that is connected to the very energy that created you, that same energy that is communicating with you in many ways.

When I hear a message, I hear a conversation taking place. I hear the message forming and write it down. This book you hold in your hands contains these transcribed messages I've received from the Universe.

It is an amazing experience to be connected so deeply and for such an extended period of time. There are not only messages, but also a divine flow of Universal energy moving through me. I'm aware that the flow of these thoughts is me and I am it, a message to you from the Universe, through me. When we listen to the messages coming through us, we connect to something greater, something bigger.

I just realized while writing this chapter that writing is what connects me to this force. Yoga and meditation have given me the opportunity to learn how to listen, given me a base.

BUT...

Writing this book is like all the things that I had ever imagined the expression of Universal energy feeling like.

The messages that need to be shared at this time are being channeled through all of us right now. Yes, this includes you! The joy I feel when I start writing is immense; I feel supported and guided and loved, and loved, and loved! I'm absolutely obsessed with this writing; when I'm away from it, I feel like a five-year old girl at a mall that has lost her mother. I scramble for paper, napkins, the backs of receipts, because there is a constant flow of inspiration coming at all times. I guess I feel gifted -- not gifted like I have more than somebody else, or am more special, or smarter, but like I have been chosen. I have been given this gift of the Universe expressing itself through me in this way at this time.

I now understand artists, understand that what they express is a message to us gifted through the artist.

Nothing else seems to matter; I have no choice but to sit here at 2:00 AM and write. The Universe has chosen me; it is becoming me, or I am becoming it. Imagine yourself as a channel of expression for what it is that the universe wishes to express at this time through you!

This is what we are.

This is what listening means: listen to the call, listen to the way in which you are being asked to express a message to the world, let it make you come alive and take you over.

Let yourself become your calling. In yoga it is called Dharma, different from destiny. Your Dharma is a gift from the Universe you have been given to share -- your cosmic duty, if you will.

You may be sitting there reading this, thinking I don't know what my Dharma is. If that's so, start to make time for listening. I've been listening for many years; however, looking back, I can see that this same energy moved through me as a teenager. I felt connected to something through writing even then.

It must find you, play with the different things that show up in your life -- those things that make you feel good, and feel that divine connection. It doesn't matter what it is; it might be a form of art, sex, food, music, talking, singing, or running, but whatever it is that makes you feel good and connects you to this effortless force of energy, do that, and begin to share it with the rest of the world. Watch (like a hawk!) for excuses and allow yourself to live the life that you have come here to live.

Your soul knows this Dharma; when you are connected to it, it comes alive – *you* come alive. You will know you're doing it because it will feel good. It's that simple.

Universe's Insight: Your life is like a jigsaw puzzle. Belief systems, media, and teachers have pieced it together. Often the puzzle is missing one piece that completes the picture; that missing piece is *you*. Your essence is missing from the creation of your life, and that's why you feel so incomplete.

Have we tricked ourselves into experiencing false terms of feeling good?

If something feels good, do it; if it stops bringing you pleasure, then stop, but trust that if it feels good that it is good—it doesn't matter what it is.

We are blessed to have as many emotions as we do, even though they don't all feel good all the time. When we are connected to this energy and are living it and expressing it in any way, the things that happen that might have felt bad or depressing before become part of the energy. There is emotion, but it becomes part of the listening, a sign to move toward what feels good. Some people are in a state of living life in a wakeful coma, and it takes a lot to show them what really feels good. Begin to listen, and be patient for the unfolding.

I've heard that it takes seven to ten years to become an overnight success. Truthfully, it does happen magically overnight for some.

Listening works the same way: practice makes perfect. Exercise your listening muscle. Detach from the outcome and start to listen to the deep calling. Start now; you don't have to sit properly on the floor with your legs painfully crossed to listen. Start right now. Just listen. Trust me; a year from now, you'll wish you had started today!

Listening Exercise

For the next week, schedule some time to sit quietly for a few minutes and listen to your thoughts. With practice, you will get to know yourself on a deeper level. Once you understand your thoughts, you will understand the manifestation of your entire life.

Universal Insight:

"If you want to change the way you think, change who you talk to. We all look for justification, especially when we are feeling the need to be right.

Notice the people that you surround yourself with. Do they always say what you need to hear, do they help you grow? What you'll start to realize is that most of the friendships you have formed tend to be ones that don't question our ego, the part that wants to be right. You get justification in these friendships, they agree with you. The Ego fights to be right while the soul enjoys being challenged because it loves being open to the expansive world of possibility."

Let me tell you a story about a woman that I know quite well (I'll call her Jamima). One day at work Jamima asked me if we could chat about something so that maybe she could see a certain situation in a different light. Her daughter had been traveling around to different countries like Australia and Thailand. In her daughter's last three weeks of traveling she was to meet up with her best friend, whose family is very wealthy. The grandmother of the wealthy friend gave both the girls six thousand dollars (!) to enjoy those last few weeks of traveling in luxury.

I instantly thought, "How awesome would that be!" But Jamima was sickened, angry, and embarrassed by this gift. After listening to her story, I realized that what I wanted to say wasn't what she wanted to hear, and that she hadn't opened the conversation into a two-way exchange. She wasn't actually hoping to view the situation in a new light. What she was looking for was more justification, and I wasn't looking like the friend that was going to agree with her. In fact, I thought and felt the opposite. The conversation suddenly became a convincing game, and I wasn't convinced.

One thing that struck me was how Jamima had sought out others to justify her perception of the situation. She had traveled in her early twenties, having backpacked and stayed at hostels, roughing it and scrounging for food. Jamima said that all of the people who she'd spoken to who had travelled the same way that she had; viewed the situation in the same light that she did.

Perhaps, I thought, if she had asked people who had traveled in luxury, she would have a broader outlook on perspectives that could help her feel more at peace about the situation. She thought that her way was the best and only way to travel, so she found people who had done it the same way in order to talk about the situation -- and they agreed with her.

In her mind she had convinced herself and many others that she was right.

So why does being right come with so much pain and anger?

The biggest delusion we have is that we think that the way we view things is the truth.

One of the biggest conversation stoppers that I have run into is when somebody says, "Well, I'm a realist, and that's just not reality." When somebody turns the conversation into an 'only one person can win' situation, what they are really saying is, "I believe my thoughts are truth and yours are worthless." If you believe that your thoughts and way of viewing the world are the only possible truths, you are going to find it hard to attract into your life anything different than what you have now.

If your mind is closed to other possibilities, there simply aren't any.

Here is something to think about that can help broaden your perspective.

There are about seven billion people on the planet at this time and that means there are about seven billion ways that the world is seen and experienced. What you believe to be true is not true for all, you might want to question -- is it true at all?

Common sense doesn't exist.

Another thing that people like to use as a quick way to win and end a conversation with others is to use the words "use common sense." Or "it's just a matter of common sense." This is one of the most bogus things anybody could ever say, and these words have a heartbreaking effect on self-confidence, especially in children.

These words hurt because they instantly belittle and degrade what the other person has thought or done.

When you think and say, "It's common sense, what your saying is… What I know to be truth is what everybody else should know and believe too.

What we forget is that in our unique makeup, we all view the world differently and we all have minds of our own.

Remember - Seven billion people, *Seven billion* perspectives and *seven billion* different beliefs of what common sense is. For example, somebody who has lived in poverty, walking eight miles for water, might have a different view of what common sense is then a person who can fill a glass of water up at the kitchen sink. One might think, it's just common sense to get three gallons of water while I'm here, and the other would find it a waste of time and energy to fill up three gallons of water and walk eight steps.

My biggest awakening was when I realized that I should never assume that anybody else in the world experiences life the same as me. Do you like to make others smaller by proving you're right, smarter, prettier etc.? If you make somebody else smaller, you become bigger right? This is what your subconscious competitor thinks.

Universe's Insight: When you think that you are better than somebody else, you create only separation.

When you spend time listening to your inner dialog, what do you notice?

Is the tune of your inner voice an overall yes or an overall no?

Does your voice sound like this, no you shouldn't have that, no, don't you dare lie down in the middle of the day; there is too much that needs to be done; no, you can't afford it; no, I'm too tired; no, I have to go home; you'll make a fool of yourself; No! No! No! I don't like that; I feel sick. Or does the overall tune sound like this: yes please; I'll have another cookie; yes we are going on vacation; you can have whatever you want, I feel good, yes, now, Yes! Yes! Yes!

Universe's Insight:

Believe it or not, you are programmed to think a certain way. You grew up with certain values, you believe certain beliefs, you were either taught to go for it or you were taught not to.

Whatever training you received, from school, church, parents, siblings, friends, peers, coworkers, media, university etc. you became the person filled with belief that you are now. So in order to start over, in order to wipe the slate of your mind clean, you must be willing to unlearn everything that you now know. Are you willing to do that? How do you unlearn?

The best way to become a master at unlearning is to see things with new eyes and ears, even taste. Start to experience things as if you have never experienced them before. Even if you have had a shower every day of your life for the last 30 years and you have a shower routine, it's always the same, nothing special. The next time you have a shower, feel the water on your skin, experience the temperature, hear it, and learn to experience everyday things in a new way.

Question things that you do, question things that you believe, question what makes you feel good, question how you feel and why. Go looking, go searching inwardly to find the beliefs that you believe and then execute them as if they were old wrapping paper. Question what you do, question the things you don't do and why you hold yourself back. The answer we're looking for is, because it makes me happy; if that isn't the answer you hear, change your belief and action right away so that you can answer any question with - because it makes me happy. Happiness is the feeling you must strive for.

We've all been in that place where we just want to be told what to do, (and yet we all hate being told what to do). But when faced with hard decisions and the I just don't know what to do's in life, we all come to this spot where we mentally throw our hands up in the air and say, I don't know what to do, give me a sign, somebody just tell me what to do.

Well, when we practice listening we discover that the answers are there, don't give away your power to anybody or anything. It's not outside of you its inside. The answer is always trying to work its way to your conscious mind where you can hear it. When you're soul gets pulled toward something you'll know, because it will feel good, you won't know whether to laugh or cry, and when you grab on to the bull's horns with both hands, hold on with all your might and know that you will fall off, you might get hurt. But you will get back up, because your soul has been waiting for this. And you know more than anything you've ever known that you must say *yes*.

Abundant energy flows to you in every way because finally you are aligned in such a way as to receive it.

I couldn't have told you this a year ago, because I'm only experiencing it now. Every time I leave my house something spontaneous happens. Every moment is filled with all that is in the flow of what I know. Every conversation becomes an inspiration; every person is a contribution to your dream.

Every song speaks your language. Suddenly everything that happens is a part of what you're doing. I'm sitting in a coffee shop right now and to my delight there is a beautiful live musician singing in the corner, just herself and her guitar. It soothes my soul in a soft sweet sort of way and as I listen... I close my eyes and say thank you, thank you for yet another gift.

The flow of gifts is abundant.

The flow of gifts is always abundant; you just need to open your awareness to the magic that's happening all around you. When you are connected to your souls' deepest desire these gifts line up so beautifully almost as if to create bridges for you. The Universe wants you to live your greatest life. When you decide, it becomes available. Everything seems to fall freely at your feet.

Universe's Insight: JUDGEMENT -- When you look around, you can't help but judge the world. Your senses lead you into a world that judges everything. The oft-repeated phrase, "Don't judge me!" is a rhetorical thing to say. You can't help yourself! You will become free when you recognize these judgments for what they are and choose for yourself not to automatically believe that they are the truth.

Fear can stop you dead in your tracks unless you are aware of what's behind that fear. Sometimes I can't help but wonder if there is something that's been driven into the human psyche that makes us believe that the hard way is better—that we have to work hard until the day we retire, that struggle and suffering are somehow a better way to live.

I had a vision today of how simple it can be if I let go of the controls. I saw myself becoming a part of nature, moving with ease toward my dreams with a deeper knowing, like how the trees seem to know when it's time to bud in the spring and the birds naturally fly south in the fall. I saw myself able to simply enjoy the moments as they passed. Suddenly, I felt a sense of fear wander into my thoughts. It seemed to tell me that I'm not ready for this, that these dreams are too big for me.

Before I listened to any more of my fear's dialog, I sat up in my bed and realized for the first time that there was a reason why this was showing up right at that moment. It had nothing to do with the dream being too big; instead, I was absolutely petrified at that moment because I realized that the dream was so very, very close.

In fact, the thought of this dream coming true was so extraordinary that it scared the shit out of me. The part of myself I have always listened to -- the part that has never been good enough, that gives up so much, that is very happy living this life, that has never stepped out of its comfort zone -- was scared! I have to say that the life that I have now is amazing and I am truly blessed, but I am ready to experience what I never believed was possible.

I'm ready and excited, and although the voice of fear is strong, my courage to recognize the untruth inside of fear vs. the truth of my soul calling me is much stronger. In the middle of my fear, I softly remind myself that I am worthy of my dreams, and my dreams are worthy of me. Let's dance together and honor the gift of being alive; experience it all, my friend. Create it, enjoy it, and live it up! It's up to you. The choice is always yours.

Your thoughts and words are constantly creating the world. Right now in this moment, how are you feeling, what are you thinking about, and how do you view the world? Do you feel loved, are you happy and healthy and feeling abundant and safe? Or is your background music that of fear, scarcity, and emptiness? Are you worried about your health? Do you believe that the world is crumbling or that people are crazy?

Do you feel that you are not safe? Are there so many frustrations that you seem to be boiling over with inner anger? It's very easy to live in a world of fear and frustration because the greater portion of messages coming from today's media and world leadership seem to have spawned from this negative place; it can seem like we have no other choice but to feel these things as well. For me, feeling safe and loved was a choosing, and I feel the most lit up when I'm choosing what feels good regardless of outside circumstances, people, and world issues.

When my son was a toddler, I remember other parents referring to their children as brats, often talking about how 'bad' they were. I made a conscious decision at that time to speak about my son in a way that was positive. I would speak to others about how wonderful he was, the sweet things he would say, and the special moments we would spend together. You create an image in other people's minds when you speak to them. When you discuss other people, places, or things, you are helping to create someone else's mental image of the world around them. I was clear on this and wanted to create my son as a wonderful little guy that people loved being around—and he is. People talk about how amazing he is, how patient and creative he is. I am blessed to have this amazing boy in my life and I tell him this all the time. If you think your kids are a handful and you speak about them this way to others, then you are creating a belief about them. In turn, that belief can create them into this way of being.

If you can get a mass people to believe in the same thing, then that belief will come to be a shared reality. I've seen this in the workplace too; one person starts talking about another person and suddenly everybody is in agreement about who this person is.

Sadly, the person being spoken about has no choice but to show up in this misconceived way because no matter what he or she really is, this is the filter they are being seen through and created by thoughts and words. Your thoughts and words are an act of creation; pay attention to what you are creating.

Every moment is an opportunity to choose a new thought, create a new life, and change the world. It's very simple. Talk and think what you dream of seeing. We have likely all heard the quote, "Be the change that you wish to see in the world" by Gandhi. Start from the inside. If you want to see love, speak love. If you want abundance, think about abundance. If you want to pursue your own dreams, ask others what their dreams are.

If you want to see peace on Earth, turn off the news and listen to someone who inspires peace. Think of this as a contribution to the entire Universe—a means of adding to the collective consciousness or the Universal mind. You are your thoughts.

What Is The Universal Mind?

The Universal Mind is the culmination of all thought that produces a global belief or habit. When we see clearly the things that we are being taught to believe, and these beliefs are believed by many, this belief becomes a reality.

If you believe that the economy is bad and a few billion other people on the planet also believe that the economy is bad, then the result of mass conscious thought is that the economy is bad; however, if you believe that the economy is good and a few billion people on the planet also believe that the economy is good, then abundance is what you will experience. This works with everything.

Think about it; if someone tells you that money will be tight, you tend to spend less. If everyone does the same, businesses make less money and may have to lay off an employee or two. The belief in a weak economy affects spending. Contributing to that weaker economy. We create what we believe.

What you come to realize is that you're always feeding the Universal Mind with your thoughts, words, and actions. It's like tuning into a channel. What channel do you want to tune into?

The Art of Relaxation and Listening to Your Craziness

Slow down, relax and let your body soften. You may notice that when you try to relax, your mind seems to become overwhelmingly busy! Over the years I have learned how to observe my own mind and experienced firsthand the craziness, the non-stop chatter going on in my head.

I like to call this the monkey mind. When you are able to sit with and observe your own craziness you can become more generous with others because this understanding of your own insanity lets you in on a huge secret: we are all crazy!

Of course there are different levels of insanity and most certainly there are levels that are frowned upon in our society but when you see your own insanity, you will also realize that everyone around you is also dealing with inner delusion **caused by the thoughts that they are having**.

This is heavy I know, but it's such a key to understanding who you are and allowing us to go deeper, past the craziness, to move past limiting thoughts and beliefs. You can choose to be great! But first you have to see who you are and what you're made of.

The greatest gift I can give you is to tell you that you're crazy. Before you make a big stink about that, let me say that you're not alone; you're on this planet called Earth with seven billion other crazy people. And we all walk around like we're normal! "I've got it together" We all try to fit into the box of normal because being crazy isn't really encouraged. You are so much bigger than that, but your bigness comes from your craziness, you need to embrace it.

So why do you ignore who you really are? Why not share that with the world? Isn't that a scary thought!

Relax and Listen Meditation

Lie down and relax deeply. Try not to move your body at all once you have found a relaxing position. Observe all the thoughts, judgments, emotions, and feelings that move through you. Try not to be active in this meditation, try not to categorize your thoughts as good or bad, truth or not truth. You will want to move your body; this is one of the things we do to avoid listening. If something is uncomfortable, you find an itch or you want to fidget. Instead, see if you can remain still; the distraction will pass. Listen to what's there, hidden in the need to move. Simply observe your mind and body. When you're done, spend a few minutes jotting down what you heard, saw, and felt.

As Michael Bernard Beckwith, founder of the Agape International Spiritual Center wisely reminds us, **"You can't hide from your secret thoughts, because they show up as your life."**

"Take the time to listen and get to know who you really are - Only then can start to live a more fulfilled life."

CHAPTER 3 MIND YOUR OWN BUSINESS

HOW YOUR COMMITMENT TO YOUR OWN HAPPINESS CAN TRANSFORM THE WORLD

"The greatest fear in the world is of the opinions of others, and the moment you are unafraid of the crowd, you are no longer a sheep, you become a lion, a great roar rises in your heart, the roar of freedom."

- Osho

It's all about feeling good! When you live a moment for somebody else, you forget who you are. In the moment this might be empathy, kindness, or compassion. But I'm talking about a different kind of living for somebody else, measured by the need to please and find approval in others. If you spend years living to please others, you forget who you are. The longer this goes on, the farther away you get from yourself. You become a zombie, numb and angry. Maybe you're changing yourself for the people you work with, your friends and your peers. Maybe you seek praise from your parents, as their disappointment is still too uncomfortable, too painful, to experience. Maybe you're holding back your true nature from your spouse, your children, or even other children's parents in an attempt to be seen as the perfect parent.

Really think about this and identify when -- or for whom -- you've stifled your personality, honesty, and truth in order to please somebody else, or even to just provoke a desired reaction. If you do something to please yourself, that's entirely different. For example, if you wear lingerie for just you and you still feel sexy in an hour, then wear it for your lover. If you wear lingerie for yourself and hate it after an hour, why would you continue to wear it for somebody else's enjoyment while you remain uncomfortable?

Take a moment to ponder…

Where else do you do this in your life?

Where do you settle for feeling uncomfortable in your own life in order to keep others happy?

Why is their happiness more important than your own?

Although it sounds selfish (and it is), if you can learn to mind your own business, you will instantly become happier. Yes, *instantly!* Did you ever notice that your level of happiness is easily measured by the people around you? It is very easy to get caught up in living for other people. You start talking to please others, and when somebody around you is having a bad day you find yourself feeling depleted.

Eventually… Your vibration changes.

If you learn one thing, learn to mind your own business. What is your business? Well, my teacher and friend Fern Hodson puts it this way: "Your business is being happy! What's my business? Happiness is my business." Is what I'm doing adding to my happiness or taking away from it? Take care of yourself and everything else will be taken care of! Fern Hodson is an energy alignment guide and EFT practitioner - there is an amazing freedom in the way that she guides her clients.

When somebody aggravates you or makes you feel pressured to do something you don't want to do, or if you find your blood boiling and you don't know why, this is a point where you have stopped minding your own business and have subconsciously crossed over to letting somebody else control your mood and your life.

So, the question I like to ask at this point is, do you like to be in control of your emotions, thoughts, and well-being, or are you willing to let everybody else and everything around you create a roller coaster that you have been strapped into that has no stop button?

It's your choice and your responsibility in every moment. First, take a deep breath and then mentally repeat, "Mind your business. What is my business? Happiness is my business."

Universe's Insight: It doesn't matter what anybody else thinks of you; your life in each moment is measured by what you think of yourself.

Are you willing to let go of controlling somebody else in order to add more happiness to your own human experience? We often get caught up in different happiness-sucking webs. The first one is allowing somebody else to affect our own inner state of joy. Imagine that you're having a spectacular day. The sun is shining warmly on you, you feel beautiful and filled with passion. It's one of those days that you feel relaxed. You've spent time in nature, you feel connected to the Universe and all its extraordinary creations. You feel healthy and your mind has been kind to you; the thoughts that you have had so far are of peace, compassion, and love. You feel a great sense of happiness; you'll even find yourself smiling throughout the day for no particular reason. This great feeling of happiness has even manifested into unexpected outbursts of joyful laughter. You like this feeling! You've waited a long time to feel this good, and it feels so wonderful. You dance to music you love. It just feels good to be in your own skin.

And then, suddenly, the mood changes; your spouse comes over to you and asks you what the hell you've been doing all day as he points to a pile of dishes that you hadn't even noticed. Suddenly you feel guilty for the time you have spent not doing anything, not meeting your spouse's expectations! Dark clouds have appeared in the no-longer sunny sky.

The world now seems cold and you feel angry, hurt, and misunderstood. Boiling now from the inside where just a few moments ago the feelings of peace and love warmed your entire being, you realize that you just allowed your spouse to completely change your vibration.

Our partners of course have their own inner battles, but should their anger become yours?

Remember these words: Mind your business!

Get back to something that makes you feel good.

Put some music on *loud*!

Dance, go back out into nature, dig your bare feet into the earth, listen to the birds singing their songs of joy, smile, let your spouse go on feeling whatever they are feeling, but let it be known that your happiness is unshakeable!

Remember that it's not about being better than the other, as the mind will want to justify things and make you right. Nobody needs to win here; you just have to stand up like a courageous, strong warrior. Stand up for happiness, joy, and grace. Happiness is your birthright. Yes, you will have days where you just feel awful; we need this contrast so that we can really appreciate what good feels like. But let it be on your own terms; become so good at minding your own business that there is nothing that anybody can say or do to you that can change your state of happiness. Remember, you are not in charge of anybody else's happiness; your happiness is your business. What's your business? This is real well being.

Universe's Insight: When you have an expectation of others, you hold them in an unreasonable space. It's unreasonable because change is constant; as human beings we are constantly changing. So when you have an expectation of others, you are secretly holding them back from their own transformation. When you have an expectation of others, your expectation will eventually

become an unmet expectation, which will lead you into disappointment. You must see that when you are disappointed, it's not anybody else's fault; you created an expectation that was unmet. Your disappointment is an emotion evoked from you not letting others be themselves. The best thing you can do in this life to support your own happiness is to learn to drop your expectations of others -- and of yourself. Let it be, let them be, let you be and you will be free.

"The snow doesn't give a soft white damn whom it touches."

~ e.e. Cummings

Live the Ultimate Dream

When you are happy, the people around you become happy just by looking at you! Happiness has grace. Happiness is the best remedy for grief, depression, and anger.

So why do we go on living lives ruled by some other definition of happiness? Why do you let something outside yourself define your worth? Why do we base our concept of beauty on what a completely airbrushed magazine model looks like?

Why do we let the world lead us into confusion about what is good for us instead of listening to what our bodies want?

Who set the scale and gets to say what is overweight? Why can't you enjoy a hamburger anymore? Why is it unacceptable to not eat for long periods of time? Why can't we take time for ourselves without thinking that we are being selfish and lazy?

Even more, why isn't it good to be selfish and lazy? Lizards are lazy and they aren't judged by their true nature. Why can't we make out in the street? Why is it more acceptable to show anger in public then to be embraced in an intimate kiss? Why do our kids shy away from dancing and singing? Even at age five it is important to look good and cool, according to some judgment from the outside world. Why don't we smile anymore?

Why is laughter so seldom heard? Why are we more comfortable in a sexy costume than we are in our own skin, why? Did you ever stop to ask, why?

It's all in your training

Why do you diet? Why do you smoke, drink, get high, take prescriptions and anti-depressants, cleanse, and run? Is it for your own enjoyment or is it to fit into a box so that you can be appreciated and accepted? Why do you exercise, why do you clean your home, why do you try to control everything?

When did you start doing so much to try to fit the part?

When did you give up on your own happiness?

Why/when did pleasing others become more important than pleasing you?

Are you willing to let go of the need to fit the part?

Do you have the courage to step out of the box that has been filled with so many rules, so many guidelines, status keepers, beauty rules, body rules, health rules, perfect family rules, bedtimes, meal times, bath times, bathroom times, financial rules?

Are you ready to not only step out of the box but also burn the box and find out who you are? Are you willing to let go of everything that you have learned to be true?

At this point in the process of realizing and manifesting your dreams let's refer to this as the unlearning stage, the peeling away of layers. This is a stage where we realize that everything that we have ever learned has been made up, created, and even scientifically proven by somebody other than you along the way.

This doesn't make it true!

If I were to say that cigarettes are healthy, would you believe me? If I could prove it scientifically that cigarettes actually kill cancer cells, would you believe me? Probably not, so why do you believe it when somebody tells you the opposite?

What you have to come to realize is that there is no truth, only what you choose to believe. And why do you need somebody else to convince you of things?

Why don't you trust yourself to know your own truth? You hand over your power by not trusting in yourself. In other words, you have handed your life over to others to control, you have no intuitive power left, something else has been running the show (your life) and you don't even know who you are, what you want, because you're living inside the box of what society says is good and right?

The problem with the box is that we lose the curiosity to question things, and just go along with the rules. But who creates the rules and why? Even more importantly, how can you reinvent your own rules?

Have the Cheesecake

You are at a restaurant. The time has come for dessert, so you look at the dessert menu and you spot your favorite thing: cheesecake! Mmm! Your initial thought when you very first lay your eyes on the word cheesecake is yes. Your whole body says yes, your mouth starts to water and you know that even though your stomach is satisfied, the answer to the question, "Would you like dessert?" is yes! Then the box that you live in starts to rethink the decision and starts chattering to you about all of the reasons that you should not have the cheesecake. Seriously, you don't need the cheesecake, you don't have any self-control, you've already spent enough money, just say no, you don't need it. And then the person you're dining with looks at you and asks if you're getting dessert. My greatest advice to you is that if you want the cheesecake, order the cheesecake! Enjoy every bite of it and be grateful.

Shiny Happy People

Let me give you an example of happy guy who knows how to mind his own business.

There is this one guy, the happiest guy I've ever seen, and I have only seen him while he is at work, so this says a lot about the guy. He said I could call him Rosco for this story. Right now while I sit here drinking my licorice tea, Rosco is taking out the garbage while singing loudly here at the coffee shop where he works. I am looking up at a chalkboard where there is a message that says, "The present is a gift."

Rosco lives this. I feel his enthusiasm for life. His happiness is contagious; he sings, jokes, and laughs with everybody that comes into the shop. He's an instant smile machine. It makes me realize how beautiful, how much of a gift it is to be happy, to be truly happy! Not because of what you have, but simply because you're happy!

When you can make somebody smile, it's a big accomplishment, but when you lift his or her spirits, it is a gift.

This is sweeter than any book you can write or read, any song you can sing, any workshop: to have a natural tendency to be happy and to make others happy just by being here. Your existence is a gift to all who encounter you! Start living your life like you are the only one you need to please. Watch what happens!

Universe's Insight: Let your light shine bright. Death is inevitable. Be alive now in the biggest, fullest way. Make a difference. Share your passion, share your dreams, and share yourself with the world now!

Get crazy, express your craziness, see where you have been suppressed and turn it into energy. Jump, scream, cry, laugh, explode. Remember how many times you've been asked to be quiet, don't cry, act normal, don't raise your voice, calm down? If you're alive, you were given the gift of emotion. Experience yourself as a smorgasbord of crazy!

I have a theory that mental illness isn't about being unbalanced.

It's about stored suppressed energy and emotion. How many people do you know who have a mental illness? Now, how many people do you think have a mental illness but don't talk about it? That makes up around 100% of the human race! As soon as you realize that you're completely messed up, you will start to break through the barriers that support your insanity!

One thing that we have become very good at in our society is pointing out when somebody else is crazy, but we never look inward to acknowledge our own craziness. You may be thinking to yourself, I'm not crazy; so and so is crazy, but I'm not crazy.

I'm not talking about the crazy we hear about every night on the news. I'm talking about the kind of craziness that everybody has, the thoughts that become beliefs, the emotions, the feeling of being right, the millions of thoughts and judgments that go through your mind every second. Humans are insane! Once you realize your own state of insanity, you will be free because you will be able to recognize the part of you that you have never been able to understand!

"Drop your neurosis." In the midst of disagreement, instead of saying this to ourselves, we tend to point the finger in the other direction and say, "You're crazy!" Instead, you should drop your own neurosis. Stop looking outside and look inward toward yourself. Your diamonds are on the inside. *Drop your neurosis! Let go of the need to be right.*

Universe's Insight: When you are tempted to point out somebody else's neurosis, stop and look toward yourself. Mentally repeat to yourself, "This is crazy, I am dropping my neurosis."

Something quite humbling happens when we acknowledge who we are and what's really going on.

We are able to be compassionate with others because we understand that in the background they are dealing with their own delusions of what's true, their own perceptions and stories, their own neurosis.

I'm not saying - lose your craziness -- that's not really possible anyway; instead, be aware of when you are creating something or pushing against something that doesn't feel good so that you can drop it and choose a more helpful thought pattern.

What's Holding You Back?

Things you aren't aware of are holding you back. I have come to realize that there are a lot of people that I steer clear of -- typically very successful, wealthy people. I was astounded at my own observation about this at my son's school fundraiser.

I noticed a woman with a Louis Vuitton bag and automatically decided that she was not a person I wanted to associate with. When I realized this, I asked myself why? Then I realized that the people I connected with the most we're the ones who had similar family and financial situations as myself.

In the past... I would steer clear of the rich people, and even make up stories about them that would justify why I wouldn't want to talk to any of them.

I realized that fundamentally, I was afraid to talk to rich people. Moreover, I looked back on my life, thought about when I feel the most intimidated; to my own amazement, it was when I was around rich people!

It totally comes from the deep-rooted subconscious belief that I'm not good enough, the "I want them to like me" syndrome.

When talking to my dear friend Fern about this discovery, she said, "It's because you want something from them. Any time you want something from somebody else there is an expectation. When there is expectation, there is a road to disappointment."

And it wasn't their money I wanted. It was simply… acceptance.

Once I wrapped my head around this, I couldn't help but wonder, does this also happen when somebody has an expectation of us that we don't meet? Absolutely! Notice the difference in a situation where somebody has an expectation of you: a relationship, job, parent, or friend. An example.

Let's say your friend and you are on a vacation together, and one of you is a morning person and one of you is a night person. The morning person gets up at six and sits in the boring hotel room for hours waiting for you to get up so you can do something together. What your friend could have done instead was go for a walk, sip on a coffee, or mingle with the early morning locals at a café; instead, your friend sat there waiting for you while the thoughts in her mind turned poisonous toward you. And now there is an awkward space held between the two of you.

Then night comes around and you want to go to a club or do something fun. Your friend just wants to go to bed. You are amazed that somebody would choose an early night instead of living it up while on vacation. You had an expectation that wasn't met, and instead of going out and enjoying the night life on your own, you stay in a boxy old hotel room twiddling your thumbs watching bad TV, or listening to the party happening outside the hotel and wishing you were taking part.

Are you getting this? This is important. When you have a subconscious or conscious expectation of somebody else, you are on the road to disappointment.

Never hold yourself back because of somebody else.

Where is your power in that?

Avoiding responsibility for your own happiness

Why do we do this? Why do we hold ourselves back from experiencing what we want and blame somebody else? Well, it was your fault we didn't do anything in Vegas, you wanted to go to bed early every night. No, it was your fault we didn't see the dolphins at sunrise, you slept until noon every day. It's my family's fault I don't have a life, my boss' fault I'm miserable, my boyfriend's fault I eat so much, and on and on and on. *Stop doing that!* Take responsibility for what you want and do it, do it every time, and do it without expectation of others.

Be prepared to go alone, meet new people and get the hell out of your comfortable little box where you have to have acceptance from everybody else. This is *your* life. Live it, own it!

While we're on the subject of happiness and freedom, let me tell you about the moment I observed and questioned how free I really was.

I was walking in the woods with my dog Harvey the other day and I took off his leash so he could run for a bit (even though it's illegal to have your dog off leash where I live. I do it anyway as I'm not really one for following the rules and I'm a sucker for seeing animals enjoying their freedom.) When I took his leash off I instantly felt his exciting sense of freedom, and then I felt a moment of sadness for the human race and myself. How many leashes was I wearing?

It was a feeling I can't describe with words, but I looked deep into the places of where I'm held back, where my freedom is leashed up. What beliefs, thoughts, and people are holding me back? Who am I obedient to, who and what has control over me? I felt sad in this moment because I questioned whether I had any freedom left at all, or worse, if

I have ever experienced true freedom at all. And then I began to wonder whose leashes am I holding onto and am I able to set them free?

I sat down on the cold, snowy floor of the Earth and watched quietly as Harvey (the beautiful animal before me) sniffed the earth, ran after squirrels that were ten times faster than he was, and marked every inch of territory that he could and when I called his name, he pretended he couldn't hear me, he was having so much fun running and chasing and marking and eating snow. He was free -- and so are we! **Remove your chains** and say *yes* to all of the things that are being offered to you.

When Harvey and I got home, I picked a card out of my animal guide cards and this is what I got:

From the Oracle Cards - Messages from Your Animal Spirit Guides

Steven D. Farmer

Copyright 2008

Published by Hay House, Inc., Carlsbad, CA

DOG - your loyalty and faithfulness is misplaced by serving too many masters.

The synchronicity of the two situations is too great not to include the rest of the writing. The Dog card went on to say...

"Whom do you serve?" is the question at hand here. When you compromise your personal integrity through misguided attempts to placate others out of fear of their disapproval or to avoid upsetting them, you deny your own inner authority and give away your power. You become their servant, and they, your masters. You allow this by assuming that another person or organization has better knowledge, power or spiritual wisdom than you, and put yourself in a "less than" position. While others may possess some of these attributes to a greater degree than you do, you can honor them as teachers -- not masters. Children may rightly look to their parents for this sort of guidance. However, as they mature, it's appropriate that the leash to their parents' authority stretches and is eventually severed. The Human error is to continue to project this parental authority onto other people and institutions, and then, either subjugate their will or act in opposition to that perceived authority. Over a number of years, you may find yourself attached to the leashes of many masters, leading you to feel fragmented and powerless. Instead, take off all those collars, and let spirit be your one true Master. Then you will experience true freedom. **~ Steven D. Farmer**

Pay Attention to the synchronicities and signs.

I had the thought, wrote it down, and then it was reinforced from the message on a card that described in depth what I was thinking. I began thinking about how many leashes I myself was wearing, and who was holding the other end.

Affirmation Exercise: Mentally Repeat, "I am free"

Close your eyes and mentally declare, "I AM FREE. I am free. I am free." Feel the freedom in these words. Visualize ultimate freedom for yourself; what does it look like?

Be one with whatever comes up for you: feelings, emotions, energy, and limitations. When we listen to our thoughts, we begin to understand who we are, how we have manifested what we have and why we feel the way we feel. Sit with this thought and see what comes up for you. Now, mentally repeat, "I alone am the creator of my life."

Universe's Insight: "Are you limited in the amount of fun you allow yourself to have? How often do you laugh? When you laugh from the depths of your soul, the Universe feels this as abundant gratitude for what is being given to you. This makes you extremely happy, and the Universe has no choice but to keep giving to you that which you are feeling."

Were You Raised to Believe in Your Amazingness, or Were You Raised to Believe Your Limitations?

Think back to when you were living with your family. What was life like for you growing up? Were you told that you could do, be, and have anything? Or were you taught to believe that life was a struggle and that your dreams were just dreams? Were you taught that it was selfish to think of yourself? When you asked for something, did you get in trouble, or did your family support you and help you find ways to manifest your dreams? Think about how your family spoke about money, dreams, possibilities; what was the energy in your home?

I have a friend who started working when she was 14, and she turned over every paycheck to her parents to help pay bills. One day, after many years of not seeing a dollar of her hard-earned money, she made a daring decision: she bought a set of pots from a salesman. They were on a payment plan: after four years, she would receive her pots. When her father came home and found out that she had spent "his" money, he lost his temper.

My friend still has subconscious guilty thoughts and fears surrounding money (as most of us do), what made all the difference in the world for her was realizing this subconscious fear around money and making a conscious decision to "let go" of the guilt! She has spent many years working at creating an abundant relationship with her money. Although it has been a lifetime work in progress. She has figured out how to manifested abundance and is wealthy.

She loves her money and her money loves her. It's never to late to change your money story.

The best part about this story is that she still has the same pots that she purchased over thirty years ago. They sparkle, and she takes great care of them. She is grateful for them and reminds herself of their value every time she cooks with them. She loves those freakin' pots!

As you look back on your life, ask yourself, "Have I been programmed to naturally manifest abundance, confidence, love, creativity, excitement, fun, laughter, pain, scarcity, fear, trust?" What's in your programming? What is your blueprint, and what would you like to tweak? In which direction would you like to take steps? What do you need to work on?

Reprogramming the Subconscious Mind

Reprogramming is all about repetition. By now you have spent time observing your own ways of thinking. You will likely have discovered that you've been repeating the same thoughts over and over again. These are the programmed thoughts that your subconscious mind has. It's like a mind trap; you can't unconsciously change these thoughts. You can, however, reprogram these thoughts by consciously choosing new thoughts once you become aware of them. It is a process, and it may take many years to reprogram some of your deeply ingrained thoughts. Be patient.

If you consider it, you have likely been repeating these thoughts for many, many years. You have created strong beliefs around these thoughts. There are clear pathways that lead to these thoughts, and now you are going to attempt to create a new pathway. You'll have to beat down the trail, clear the bushes and get rid of the rubble.

This is one of my favorite quotes By Henry David Thoreau:

"As a single footstep will not make a path on the earth, so a single thought will not make a pathway in the mind. To make a deep physical path, we walk again and again. To make a deep mental path, we must think over and over the kind of thoughts we wish to dominate our lives."

Henry David Thoreau was born in 1817, and this wisdom has been passed down over many years.

Programming the mind is not a "New Age" theory. It is the wisdom of the most successful, spiritual, happy people who have lived.

Buddha said, "Your thoughts are everything, what you think, you become."

Albert Einstein said, "You cannot solve a problem with the same mind that created it."

Take the time to get to know thy-self and don't be afraid to reprogram your mind. This is the message they have all been passing down for ages, despite the powers that be.

Maybe it's because these powers don't want us to understand our own power so that we will obediently submit to the leashes they hold.

Imagine if we were taught in school, the power of understanding your own mind and reprogramming it. How would your life be different? My theory is: If you don't take steps to reprogram your own mind it's almost for certain that it will be programmed by some other means.

Universe's Insight: "Follow your dreams - We call it following your dreams because that is precisely the point. A dream or a persistent thought is something calling you to it; your job is to follow it."

"Mind your own business! Make yourself happy; what's your business anyway? You can't fix anybody else's un-happiness."

CHAPTER 4 GET OUT OF THE BOX

A PERSON WITH A FREE MIND CAN FREE THE ENTIRE UNIVERSE

While I was staying at a bed and breakfast called Between Friends in Vancouver, I enjoyed morning conversations with the owner, Simone. We were having a chat one morning about how children yearn to please their parents, and how they begin at a young age to let their strong, rebellious 'knowing' go.

We do so because being loved and appreciated by our parents is a sweet and comfortable place, and to feel unloved even for a second by our family feels like being tossed out of the nest. A child only knows love; because of this, he will leave his own strong will for a moment of acceptance.

This is where the road to a never-ending, boxed-up life begins. Simone called it the "false cookie." We teach our kids at a very young age that when they do as they are told, that we will love them and that when they are good, we give them a cookie. When a child goes against the rules, says no, throws a temper tantrum, won't go to bed, or spits out what mom has cooked, he is reprimanded.

Here is our first box. Let's call it the **DO WHAT YOU'RE TOLD OR I WILL TAKE MY LOVE AWAY** box. Wouldn't you agree that as human beings, we would do anything to feel the soft touch of love?

We came from love -- it's what we crave.

So when you feel the pain of your parents seemingly taking their love away, you subconsciously decide to do what you are told.

Before we know it, we become children who sit properly, speak correctly, and eat everything on our plates -- even if we're full or don't enjoy what we're eating. All, for Acceptance and Love

And then we wonder why, as adults, we can't intuitively figure out when we're full, why we overeat and feel undernourished. We go to bed at proper times, eat at the same times every day whether we're hungry or not, we say our please and thank you, and if we forget once, we feel the cloud of disapproval.

I think it's fair to say that by the time you turned five or six you were pretty much programmed to do what everybody else wanted from you. In the meantime, what happened to your will, that deep desire inside of you that would scream when unhappy, cry for the right food, stomp when somebody said no? Where did your power go? Forget about the approval cookie, go make your own batch of cookies and approve of yourself!

Approve of everything you are, everything you want: when you get tired, go to bed; when you get hungry, eat. Re-create yourself and make your will strong.

As We Get Older...

Do the people in your life add to or take away from your experience of feeling good? An easy way to tell if you're in a box that doesn't serve you is to ask yourself, "Am I happy?"

If you're not, chances are good that you have put yourself into a box where somebody else thinks you should be.

You will notice when you're around certain people that you feel happy, good, and loved. You will have the feeling of belonging. On the other hand, when you're around people and you feel uncomfortable, unhappy, or full of judgment and criticism, you are probably trying to squish yourself into a box that is not supporting who you really are.

Of course, many of these situations are unavoidable in life, but the ability to be aware of how you are feeling is a gift because you are then able to choose something different. If it doesn't feel good, why do it? Your duty is to walk in the direction that brings you joy.

Make that your commitment. You may find it helpful to start planting ideas in your mind such as, "I choose to walk a life of happiness because I am worth it." People may judge me, and that's ok! I still have the courage to be me."

Activate the Momentum of Feeling Good

Altered States of Consciousness

The song "I Want a New Drug" by Huey Lewis and the News has played in my mind for many years. And it's because somewhere deep down -- locked away, chained up, and boxed in -- was this other me. I knew that there was more to life. I wanted a taste of something else. I didn't consciously realize that there was something more, but I could feel the pull; my greater self knew that there was a destiny, a reason for being here beyond what I had experienced so far.

When I'm writing, it's like being on a drug. It's the greatest thing ever! In the beginning I just liked expressing my thoughts on paper. Now, when I immerse myself into writing, hours, days, even weeks and months go by without effort. I am completely taken; the world as I have always known it fades and I become alive from the inside out. I am the book I'm writing -- the book and I are not separate. I can't sleep. Eating is optional, and remembering other things that need to be done becomes difficult.

All I can think about is when I will be able to write again. Everything around me, all conversations and interactions, become a contribution to my next writing session. I am constantly taking notes and dreaming about the life of a writer. I have found the drug that makes me whole, a drug where nothing else matters. This is my obsession. Sometimes I wake up and can hardly open my eyes because I have been squinting into my computer the whole night, and yet there is this vibration of being utterly and completely alive! I can't wait to get back at it. It's the perfect hit.

This is what I want for you, my friend: find what gives you that rush, whatever it is, and let it take over your entire being. Let the boxes and limitations in your life fade away like smoke and focus all of your energy there, for that is what you are here for. You'll know when you've found your drug because you will lose yourself. It'll take over your life and it'll be effortless; you'll feel like some magical force is carrying you!

Just yesterday I was sitting on my patio listening to the birds singing and saw a bird perched at the top of a spruce tree. I thought, wow what freedom you have, your view of the world must be extraordinary. And then another bird, a raven I believe, showed itself in all its beauty, flying lazy circles in the sky above me, looking almost as if it were floating. I thought to myself, I'm flying. I can see the world through the eyes of a raven because I have opened the cage door and flown, I am unbound, and I am limitless.

I imagine what a world it would be if we could all be like that—if all people were flying high, unbound by the fear, unbound by the chains that hold us down when we try to soar, unleashed by the thoughts tethering us inside, freed from that box that tries to make us all the same. I hope that you find what frees you. A bird doesn't wait to see if everybody approves of where it's going; it simply spreads its wings and flies.

Anything that you believe to be true is a limitation.

Anything that you strongly believe to be true is a limiting belief. To think that you know the truth about anything is to be ignorant in the knowledge that everything is in constant flux. The eyes of a child exploring its world for the first couple of years seem to be windows into a world of pure amusement. Although I would love to be able to say that I know what children think, I simply cannot. But what I do know is freedom.

When you were a baby and you looked at a tree for the first time, you saw this huge amazing thing, bugs crawling everywhere, rough bark, and leaves that fall with the wind. You could spend hours exploring this one thing. But as soon as your parents taught you the word tree and pointed to it, you lost the ability to see the magnificence because now you 'knew' what the tree was. You were proud in your knowing and every time you saw a tree you would point and say "tree, tree!" Your parents would clap their hands, and you began to realize that if you memorized this world around you and learned it like everyone else, you would receive praise and Love.

As soon as we are sure of what something is or presume to know the truth about anything, we lose our ability to experience the world as a miraculous and magical place of wonder. When we start to see beyond a constructed truth, we see a much bigger picture, and our fight to be right disappears because we realize there is nothing to be right about.

There is not one thing that I can speak about as if I know the truth about it (and am very cautious when somebody speaks with such conviction.)

There is only what has been made up by somebody along the way. You can choose what you want to believe to be true; I tend to avoid constructing truths simply because I love to bathe in the wonder! The only thing that I truly know is how I feel.

I can only share the truth that comes from my experiences. Allow yourself the freedom to start living a life where you feel life experiences instead of being *taught* life experiences.

Own Your Own Greatness

My son Noah has always amazed me with his fearlessness. He is as much a teacher to me as I am to him, if not more. We were sitting at the mall today for lunch and he blew my mind with his words of wisdom. I have a radio interview in a week and I keep coming up against feelings of fear and procrastination.

But when I ask myself what I'm afraid of, nothing sticks out; I'm just flat-out nervous.

Today is the day of Noah's school talent show. He is dancing to the song "Power" by will.i.am and Justin Beiber. Noah has no fear at all about being on stage, or about meeting people or asking for what he wants, for that matter. He has been talking about being an actor since he was three, and we have just recently set him up with an agent. In fact, he attended his first audition last week. He had no fear.

None. He just did his thing! So I told him at lunch that I had a radio interview coming up and that I was nervous and scared.

"Why? That's so awesome," he responds.

"I know! I'm excited and nervous. How do you do it?" I asked him.

"Easy," he says. Just pretend you're having a conversation with your best friend, don't think about the billions of people listening."

I love that he's used the word *Billions*. He finished, quickly gulping down the rest of his pizza. The best advice I've ever gotten about overcoming fear came from my seven-year old son in the mall, eating pizza and cookies on a busy Wednesday at lunchtime! Messages, masters, and miracles come at unexpected moments; be ready to receive these gifts.

I realize now after pondering this for a bit that my fear came from the idea that what I say on a radio show, or in a workshop—or write in a book—has to be something that pleases everybody. What if I say something wrong? What if I am asked a question that I can't answer? What if people don't like the sound of my voice, or even worse, don't like me? Ahhhhhhh!

Then I remembered my son's wise words. It's not about them! I totally got it! What I want to say is what I want to say. I want to share what I'm passionate about and inspire others to do the same. I want to be free from the subconscious torture of my thoughts that say I can't do it. I want new experiences. I want to say yes to everything! I want to be fearless in the face of self-doubt. I want to live without being held back in any way. I want to feel confident and successful, like I could take on the world. Just like my son said, I want to do it for me.

Start sorting through the thoughts and beliefs that you have—you have many! In fact, you are a big ball of energy filled with thoughts and beliefs. It is these thoughts and beliefs that create who you are; your strongest beliefs are your boxes. Your religion, your health, your financial situation, the way that you judge and view the world help create your personality. Your character is formed by your thoughts, beliefs, and who you aim to please. So, who is that? Who are you?

In order to get out of the box, you have to realize that you're stuck in the box to begin with.

I am so sick of the way that people walk around programmed to think they must be perfect!

It totally sickens me the way we are told to eat properly, drink properly, walk properly, talk properly, be proper, don't do this, don't do that. When I people-watch on a busy street, I see a bunch of messed up human beings all trying to fit into a box that society says is acceptable.

Beautiful women sucking their stomachs in.

People's lips moving who aren't saying anything.

Men trying to be macho.

As I watch hundreds of people walk by, I see one girl who has the courage to be different. She's dressed colorfully, is singing a song, and even though everybody looks at her askance, she keeps going, even adding a little dance in her step. Her smile is bigger than any smile I have seen. Her happiness comes from her ability to please herself without attachment to what others think. I bet most of the people on that same street wished that they could join in, wished they could feel that kind of freedom. Unfortunately, they seem to be on some sort of invisible leash, trained by society to be obedient.

When you are minding your own business, you give other people permission to mind their own business, too. You can still be a compassionate, generous human being while you live for you! Do you think Gandhi did what he did because he wanted to please others? Do you think he woke up everyday and wondered, "What will they think of me?" No, Grande stood up and lived his life with absolutely no fear at all; he was not interested in what anybody else thought or said. He lived to please himself! Indeed, his calling was grand and made him a catalyst for a new way. He started a revolutionary movement!

Just like the Beatles, Buddha, Madonna, Einstein, Donald Trump, Oprah, Martin Luther King, Nelson Mandela, and many more. None of these people aimed to please anybody else. They moved powerfully in the direction of their dreams and let nothing stop them.

Universe's Insight: "Whether your message, passion, and true nature is something that people agree with or not isn't important; what's important is that you do it because it makes you happy and it adds to a joyful experience of *your* life."

"First... You gotta realize that you're in the box!"

CHAPTER 5 - ASK

THE SECRET TOOL USED BY THE MOST SUCCESSFUL PEOPLE IN THE WORLD

When you ask for what you want, the Universe conspires to make that happen!

We are often unconscious about what we are asking for. Whether we want it or not, the Universe hears our desires and starts bringing them into form. The other rule of the law of attraction is to ask from a clear place, meaning that the channel or connection from which you are asking is not fuzzy. Think of a radio; as you're turning the dial, there is a lot of static (like your mind most of the time.)

When you tune into the one station that you want to hear, it comes through clearly. This doesn't mean that the other stations don't exist; in fact, all of the chatter, static, and other stations are still emitting their signals as strongly as before. The difference is that you have tuned into one station.

When you do this, you tune into the channel that you want to focus on or ask from. This is what you are doing when you go into an alpha state meditation (we will practice this technique in chapter six).

I have been experimenting with this form of meditation for many years. The Alpha state meditation is the natural state from which children manifest. Since I started using the Alpha state meditation, I have created many miracles in my life, and the results are fast. When you become clear about who you are and what you want, you enter a place where you deny yourself nothing. When you ask from this clear and abundant place, your dreams come to life!

Are you ready to receive and say yes to what starts pouring into your life after you ask? When you become a master at consciously asking for exactly what you want, the things that you ask for come to you rapidly. Be ready!

How Do You Ask For What You Want?

Practice listening first to what it is that you really want. An easy way to do this is to notice the things that you don't want, experiences that you don't like; things that you don't want to go through again. Our brains are trained to notice the negative things -- we are much better at complaining and picking out what we don't want than we are at finding the positive side to things and the beauty in life. So an easy way to get clear on what you *do* want is to first get clear on what you *don't* want.

If you know that you don't like struggling to pay your bills or make ends meet, maybe financial abundance would serve you better. Or, let's say you've been in a relationship that doesn't elevate you, or perhaps the other person treats you negatively, and deep inside of you is a longing for a passionate relationship. You crave affection, fun, and love. You have experienced what you don't want, so now you can see the contrast, the opposite: you can see clearly what you do want. Sometimes we become stuck in a world of getting more of what we don't want, but if we can learn to use these not-so-great experiences as a key to figuring out what we do want, nothing less than miracles are available.

Listen to the vows that we make on our wedding day:

"Till death do us part."

If this isn't a stuck situation, I don't know what is.

I love how Abraham Hicks, through Ester Hicks, explains this when Abraham Hicks says,

"A better vow might be one that states, 'I like you right now, let's see what happens."

You can find more delightful insights from Esther and Abraham on the website AbrahamHicks.com or by calling 803-755-2299.

By taking our wedding vows, a certain amount of our freedom is unconsciously signed away. How could you possibly know that what you feel on the day of your wedding is going to be the same until the day you die? But still ten, twenty, even sixty years later you get up, do the same thing, keep your thoughts tucked away in the back of your mind so that nobody knows how you feel. You settle for what you have because you have been told that you are blessed, that you are lucky to have what you do, and you've told yourself that you are committed to this until the day you die.

Oh God, just writing this makes me want to throw up! What the hell are we doing? Are you willing to settle for an unhappy life where you become numb to your own thoughts and desires? And instead of saying what you want, you just survive, lose your magic, and become old and angry. I for one am not willing to waste a moment of my life in this way.

When did you stop asking for what you want?

When did you stop believing that you were worthy of the kind of love that you see in the movies?

I remember the first time somebody said to me, that's not real, it's Hollywood; love like that doesn't exist.

I believed that for a long time. But I have experienced that kind of love, I've seen it in the world, I've found it with my husband.

I believe that it exists. When you have the thought that you would like something more, stay with it. Don't brush it off as some fantasy that will never come true. Write it down, daydream about it. Believe that you are worthy of ultimate happiness, extraordinary love, fun, financial abundance, your dream home, dream life, joy, joy and more joy!

BELIEVE THAT YOU ARE WORTHY OF IT! ANYTHING!

Universe's Insight: Intentions can help strengthen yourself and others. When you look at somebody with the intention to send them love, even meditating on a mental picture of a loved one with positive intentions from far away, you can actually strengthen them. When you send a nasty thought or intention to somebody, you

weaken them. **This is why it is important to be aware of the people that you play with; make sure they lift you up, support you, and strengthen you. The power of the mind is far beyond what we can grasp.**

Intention Setting is a Form of Asking

Years ago I read the book *The Power of Intention* by Dr. Wayne Dyer. It was the first time I had explored the idea of intention setting; now I use this method of setting an intention every day, and it has helped me remember who I am and how I want to live.

What is intention? Intention is an aim or plan. I often start my yoga classes with a setting of intentions. This gives the person practicing a chance to think about what they have come to class for, what has brought them to their mat today. It brings awareness to their desires in the present moment. When I set my intention in the morning before I get out of bed, I say to myself, today is a miracle; I am so blessed to be here now. My intention for the day is to move toward what brings me happiness. I prefer to step away from conversations and people that bring me down so that I may move in the direction that brings me the most happiness.

When we are detached from our own intentions the rest of the world seems to run our lives and we forget what is important to us individually. Intention is a powerful tool in manifesting your life as you wish it to be. Throughout the day my intention may change; when my son is yelling my name and I'm cooking breakfast and the dog needs to go for a walk and I can't even get myself together long enough to get out of my pajamas and into clothing for the day, I may take a deep breath and set my intention for patience, calm, and peace. You see, whatever it is that I set my intention on is where I am, and that's what I get. Setting an intention is an instant switch. The 'easy' button for the mind and body.

I also use the power of setting intentions when I am healing. I practice a form of distance healing called Intentional Intuitive Healing, and I have seen magical things happen. For more on the type of healing I do, go to AstraLily.com

I have gotten higher marks on exams, not from studying more but from saying my intention is to do my best, to play 100% in this game of life and finish what I have started.

My intention also helps me remember why I am doing something. It reminds me of what my goal is so that I can keep moving in that direction.

Sometimes when I'm writing I will set an intention to write a certain number of words in one sitting. It doesn't matter what it is; I always reach my intention.

Intention-Setting Morning Exercise

When you wake up in the morning, before you crawl out of bed, take three long deep breaths. Take a moment to picture your goal for the day or moment; maybe you have a long-term plan that you're working towards. Get a clear picture of what you want and mentally repeat your intention three times. Start with the following sentence:

My intention is to _____.

It might be as simple as being at peace, or writing 3000 words, giving ten hugs, making a certain amount of money, or finishing a project. Whatever your honest intentions are when you mentally repeat them, it's like your subconscious mind is talking to your conscious mind. And best of all, you're aware and listening to what you really want to create.

Do this every day for fourteen days and see what unfolds.

Universe's Insight: Worthiness - You are worthy. Let your approval come from within. Be aware of your seeking of worthiness from others. You can look at worthiness in two different ways: you are worthy of your dreams, and your dreams are worthy of you.

Do I believe that I deserve to have what I dream of?

Am I worthy of the company I keep?

Sometimes in life we might start to think that our dreams are just too big and dismiss them as that, just a dream. Look closely at what it is that you daydream about. Start to follow your dreams and know that you are deserving of them. You are worthy of all of the blessing that life has to offer. Accept who you are -- look at your imperfections and see them as perfections. Diplomas, employment, family status, body shape -- all of these are things that people use to judge you; if you don't meet their criteria, you may feel insecure and unworthy. Instead, I urge you to take a look at what makes you *you* and ask yourself, are they worthy of me? It's time to create your own scale of what worthiness is. Know that life is always unfolding and that your life is unique. You no longer need validation from others to stay centered in a place of worthiness.

Universe's Insight: When making the conscious choice to ask the Universe for what you want, phrase things in a positive way. I can. I am. I love it when, It arouses me when.... If you can think it, it can happen.

The Reason That Most People Don't Have What They Want Is Because They Don't Know What They Want.

Imagine being a genie and waking up from a long sleep to grant three wishes to a very lucky person; however, the wishes were scattered confusing, contradictory.

I want a big mansion, or maybe a small self-sufficient house with a maid --no, I should be able to clean up after myself and my family. How about a garden! Actually, I hate gardening. It should have large rooms for every occasion, but really, just two bedrooms should do. An infinity pool in the Hawaiian mountains, oh, and a wood stove to cook in, or maybe a big luxurious kitchen.

How difficult would your task of granting these wishes be? This is the problem we see within ourselves. Our thoughts are confusing to the Universe because we are not clear on what we really want. The law of attraction is like your own personal genie, but when you are confused and unclear about what you want, the Universe sits back and says, I'm just going to wait until you figure out what really matters to you. In our everyday lives, this creates a fuzzy manifestation channel so things take a long time to happen, or they don't happen at all.

Another common misstep when trying to make a dream a reality is hesitation. When you receive inspiration or a moment of clarity and the Universe brings you an opportunity—a door to open, or the first step to take towards your goal—something happens; you become filled with fear and say no. You hesitate. The Universe thinks you don't really want what you say you want, so the flow stops and you go back to your old ways.

Practice saying yes to the things that are being offered to you. For one day try to say yes to absolutely everything that is offered to you.

Work your way up to a week, then a month.

Let yes become a natural occurrence, and the Universe will start bringing you more things to say yes to!

You see; this is about consciously co-creating your life.

Acknowledge Fear

Fear is something that we can't just press a button to stop. Fear is part of who we are. Fear can even be helpful at times, as being connected to fear can actually help keep us out of trouble, or tell us when it's time to go. As unlikely as it sounds, fear can at times be a friendly helper.

On the other hand, fear can also run the show. If you watch the news, read the newspapers, or keep pace with political elections, you will see very quickly that we are preprogrammed to live in fear. This is one of those Big Boxes that we have subconsciously shoved ourselves into. We all carry this long list of fears with us:

- **Fear of not having enough**
- **Fear of losing what we have**
- **Fear of animals**
- **Fear of being hurt**
- **Fear of not being good enough**
- **Fear of running out (lack of)**
- **Fear that others won't like you**
- **Fear that you can't do it**
- **Fear of being unhealthy**
- **Fear of dying**

Take a moment to mentally add any fears to this list that come up for you.

Universe's Insight: Although there are many things to fear, what you fear the most is your own power, your own greatness. It has become easier for you to dumb yourself down to fit in than to be great at who you are.

Once you become a master at listening, you can see, feel, and hear the thoughts of fear when they creep in. So instead of fear stopping you, you can stop it and step beyond it.

One way that I play this game is to use affirmations when I notice fear getting in the way of my success. I listen, acknowledge, say thank you, and replace the fear with a more helpful thought. For example, while writing this book (which has been a dream of mine for almost 20 years), many changes have taken place. There are days when I feel confident, sure, and totally connected to what is flowing through me and out of my hands. Then there are days that I wake up in fear that I have the dreaded writer's block, and my thoughts start turning in the direction of what am I doing, what was I thinking, I can't do this, nobody wants to read this stuff, I'll never make it as an accomplished writer.

Then with the watchful eye of my inner hawk, I stop and I listen to the craziness running through my mind. I have realized that in acknowledging these thoughts and replacing them with positive ones, I am helping to create the magic I want in my life. I realize that the thoughts playing in my head are not in alignment with what I want, so I reach for a thought that would be more helpful in accomplishing my goal. I picture meeting Louise Hay and having book signings all over the world. I ask for the connection to the source that so freely flowed through me yesterday and I start choosing thoughts like, I can do this, I can't wait for this to happen, of course I'm nervous and scared, but that's ok. Sit down and write for 10 minutes; this is your golden ticket. This is what you love to do. You are an amazing writer. And I set an intention: my intention is to be a bestselling author. You know what authors have to do? Write!

Universe's Insight: You have been taught not to ask for what you want. You have been led to believe that asking for what you want is greedy. You are scared to ask for the extraordinary things that you dream about. You think it's easier not to ask at all than to become disappointed. You await disappointment; you've become accustomed to it and you wait for it. Humans seem to constantly manifest disappointment. It is now time for you to overcome these habits and beliefs. Have a clear channel from which to ask. Powerfully and clearly ask for what you want. Trust that all will come.

What Is The Law Of Attraction?

I asked a guy at work one day if he understood the law of attraction. He answered with a yes and went on to tell me about how opposites attract, about how magnetically opposite ends of magnets stick together. We have a subconscious way of thinking that everybody knows and understands exactly the same way as we do. I was humbled that I got to explain the fascinating law of the Universe to him.

The law of attraction is the simplest law to understand: it states that what you think about becomes your reality, and what you focus on will come to be. You are the magnet, and what you think about comes to you. Your life is a manifestation of your thoughts, so if you're thinking that you would love to go to Hawaii, but the thoughts around the Hawaii trip are not in alignment with what you want (I'll never be able to get time off work, I'll never have enough money, I can't make it happen) then you will create situations that require you to work more, you won't save money towards the trip, and you will not end up going to Hawaii.

Every thought that you have is a creation. Read that line again!

Become aware of what your thoughts are up to; they can be very sneaky. Keep listening and choose to focus on what you *do want* instead of what you *don't want*. Remember that your mind has been trained to focus on what you don't want, so be easy on yourself when you begin this journey of understanding yourself.

I saw the law of attraction in action one day while I was playing a game of snakes and ladders with my wonderful son. He started telling the dice what he wanted to roll. If he said, "Come on three!" he would roll a three. He was hitting all the ladders and climbing through the game at winning speed while I just slithered my way down a snake here and there. I love to see my son win; I can see the confidence building as he moves toward the finish line. But suddenly he starts talking to the dice in a different way, saying what he doesn't want to roll to avoid landing on a snake. So if he said, "Please, no five, don't be a five," he'd roll a five!

It doesn't matter what context you put your asking in, the Universe only hears it as a request. He's focused on a five, give him a five. The Universe doesn't hear the negatives or the don'ts, it only senses the energy of what you're focused on. It wants to bring that to you. I know it sounds crazy, but he started rolling what he didn't want and down the snakes he went over and over again.

I ended up winning the first game and said to him "Noah, don't think about what you don't want, focus on what you do want, only tell the dice what you want, tell the game that you want to win, not that you don't want to lose." And you can probably predict what happened next: he won the next two games, often rolling the number that he asked for to land on ladders and avoid the snakes. It was like watching a miracle happen right before my eyes!

The Law of Attraction is just as much a law as the law of gravity. If you throw a ball into the air, it will fall to the ground. If you think about something repeatedly and focus your conscious energy on it, it <u>will</u> come to you. Although this sounds simple, the Law of Attraction is misunderstood and therefore not used properly, as people are often <u>un</u>aware of what their subconscious thoughts are creating.

Whose Dream Are You Living?

When you are unaware of what your dream is, you walk around envying what other people have because you don't believe that you can have it. Perhaps you don't even really want what you've been trained to believe that you need. Have you been programmed in this life to live, have, be and do what everybody else is, has, does, and lives? Sometimes it feels like we are zombies in our own life: numb to feelings, emotions, and desire. We have all conformed in many ways to fit into what is acceptable in our society; however, we are constantly striving to do it better than everybody else.

This is the biggest delusion that leaves us in a continuous state of feeling not good enough, of not having enough. We carry large debts to keep up to our subconscious need to be average. But the biggest crime of our time is that we have stopped dreaming. When you stop dreaming, you become numb, and when you become numb, you're not happy—and when you're not happy, being alive isn't very much fun! So have the courage to stand out and create your life, live your dream, be different, be you!

So—what is your dream?

What do you really want more than anything else? What is the first response that springs to mind? When I was asked this question at a friend's house one night, the answer was clear: "I want to be a famous author." After answering, I started to question my answer. My mind started pondering the things I would have to give up in order to get what I really want. Then I had the "Aha!" moment. Why do I think that getting what I want means that I would have to give something up? Can't I simply add to what I already have? Greatness isn't achieved by believing and pre-determining what you can't have; instead, it has more to do with believing that you can have it all. Do you truly believe that you can have it all? That is the state of mind from which your brilliance will shine and manifest.

Not only do your thoughts create your life, they can actually predetermine your life: how you're going to feel, when you'll be tired and why, what time you'll eat, sleep, when you'll have kids, who you'll talk to, how your day will be. You secretly predetermine your whole life.

Now, wouldn't you like to get into the habit of noticing your predetermining thoughts that are limiting you? These limiting thoughts keep you where you are; they have you play a small game. But, the cool thing about noticing these small limiting thoughts is that now you can act to choose predetermined thoughts that create a bigger picture, that challenge your comfort zone.

You can predetermine how you're going to feel, how much energy you will have today, how little sleep you need, how healthy you are, how much love you will receive and give—predetermine the outcome of a conversation, the outcome of any situation.

Consciously reprogram your life by consciously predetermining how you want it to go. My beautiful friend and life coach, Jean Roberts, gave me this insight one day when we were talking about being tired. She was planning a party and had a very full week, so I said, "Will you be too tired? Maybe we should come at seven so that you can have a little rest before we get there." She answered with the brilliant answer, "I'm sick of predetermining when I will be tired; we predetermine everything. On Monday, I already know how tired I'm going to be on Friday." From this insight came an enlightening addition to what I already knew.

Universe's Insight: "Your mind has been led to see the world in a certain way, to eat certain way, to parent a certain way, to look a certain way, to talk a certain way, to fear, to hide, to settle, and to dream a certain way. If you want to start living your dream, you first have to realize why you can't. See what is holding you back. Only then can you move beyond your programmed way of being into a limitless way of being. Asking for what you want is a muscle that weakens very quickly if it's not used. The more you ask, the stronger and faster the results.

Why are you so scared to say what you really want? When you were a child you would kick and scream for what you wanted; now you talk yourself out of it before you even ask. You have become a coward to your dreams and desires.

Don't sit on your butt waiting for the change to happen. Dream again, do whatever it takes to get yours, cash in your golden ticket and use your gift to create financial balance on this planet. It is time to restore the balance of all the money on the Earth. Imagine doing what you love effortlessly; it is your duty to be wealthy and restore balance, not only so that you can have the things that you want, but to balance out the global finances of Earth!

Imagine how generous you could be and how many more people you could help out if you had lots of money? Money needs to be spread out into the hands of people like you. Using your gift will create a constant and abundant flow of money. You will be completely taken care of. It's a big dream and a big destiny, but imagine if I were to tell you that your interest in this book is helping to bring balance to the financial system in your planet? You can do it just as easily as anyone else. Do this for each other—an abundant world for all.

Stand up and use what you have been given, let it explode out of you. It is your birthright to share your most authentic self in this life. You have an extraordinary gift waiting to be realized and used to restore financial balance—so use it! What is your gift?

Universe's Insight: One percent of the people on your planet are holding all the money and power. There is enough for everyone! Find what makes you come alive and do that, share it with the rest of the world, and change the way your global money is distributed."

When I received this message from the Universe, I saw this vision and listened to this thought. For the first time I looked at money as something that is out of balance on our planet, and in order to create balance, everybody needs to use the full potential of his or her gifts to create financial abundance. When the money of the world can be spread out to more people, financial balance on our planet will be attained.

I teach a restorative yoga class. This class is all about listening to your body and asking for what you need and want to make your body as comfortable as possible. I regularly remind people to ask for what they need to make the posture that they are in ultimately comfortable.

People who are used to modern yoga classes are used to pushing harder, pulling their face closer to their legs to get more of a stretch. So when I explain at the beginning of a class that the next hour and fifteen minutes is going to be all about deep relaxation and listening to the needs of your body and asking for what you want, and that most postures are held for fifteen to twenty minutes, most people look at me with in confusion.

Throughout the class I keep reminding people to relax deeply, to ask for assistance when they feel the need to change the posture to suit their needs. I walk around the room offering blankets, pillows, bolsters, and blocks to support their needs.

I like to give people a line that I came up with in my restorative yoga teacher training with Tianne Allen in Vancouver. I say, "If you were going to a massage therapist for a massage, you wouldn't jump on the massage table and try to massage your own body, so let me assist you in becoming so relaxed that your body feels completely supported."

Although I can see that most people enjoy the practice, there are only a couple that will attempt to get my attention by calling me over, waving a hand, or simply making eye contact. In the restorative yoga classes, something amazing happens when somebody has the courage to wave me over for assistance.

Suddenly… three or four people are all waving me over to assist them, too. It's as if this first person to ask for what he or she wants gives the rest of the class permission to ask for what they want.

Just like in life, in a relationship, when one person asks for what they want, it gives the other person an opportunity to share what it is that they need as well. This is the starting point of freedom. The lesson here is to get to a place where you are listening to your body and hearing what it needs in each moment—because what is comfortable in this moment isn't necessarily comfortable five minutes later. It's up to you whether you want to stay in an uncomfortable position or change it to suit you better.

I have learned so much about what people are willing to put up with instead of simply making an adjustment and nurturing their needs. In life, why do you settle for what is uncomfortable when you can choose to change it and make it more perfect? Somewhere deep down you believe that you don't deserve perfect, so you settle for ok and uncomfortable. Be responsible for asking for and creating your own happiness, bliss, love, abundance, fun, and ultimate comfort.

One thing I realized is that sometimes we think other people -- especially people close to us -- should be able to read our minds and give us what we want without ever telling them. This is a recipe for disaster. Never assume that anybody knows what you want unless you tell them.

Another reason you don't ask for what you want is because of a deep rooted issue that, subconsciously, you don't believe that you are worthy of something better. You have learned to settle. Whether it's pain in your body, depleting

relationships, a job that robs you of your happiness --
whatever it is, you stopped believing that you are worthy of
anything better, so you stopped asking. When you ask for
what you want, you also risk bringing attention to yourself;
if you're not a confident person, chances are you don't want
to attract attention to yourself.

This is one of the rules of nurturing. You must be willing to
attract attention. This is what you want anyway; your soul
has been shouting at you to pay attention. It is trying always
to bring you to a higher state of being. When you practice
asking for what you want in life and adjust things when they
could be even just a little bit better, you become free -- and
the people around you learn that asking for what they want
is valuable too.

**Universe's Insight: "Life is long. How many times have
you heard the saying "life is short"? Well life isn't really
short, is it? Actually it's quite long. If you think about all
of the things you have done so far in your life, you might
start to see how big and long life is. Enjoy each moment,
each unfolding. Live now, then now, then now, and then
now. Practice presence in each moment."Spiritual Gift -
Your Golden Ticket**

What is a spiritual gift? You were born with a special
something. You were born to share this special something
with the world. When you are in alignment with this gift and
bring it to life, you will be taken care of in all ways. People

who struggle through life have one thing in common: they don't see the value in who they are and what they have to offer. They are trying to fit the shoe that others are wearing, and that shoe just doesn't fit -- or perhaps they have lost touch with their gift altogether.

When you know your gift and are using it and sharing it, life flows easily because you are listening to the calling of your soul, a soul that has always known who you are. Your spirit is the part of you that never dies and never will. It carries your essence, and your essence is the vibration of truth that belongs to you. The Universe wants you to use your essence to navigate through this life; it is what you have been given to thrive. When you use your gifts, the Universe rewards you. Your soul understands this and wants to thrive. Not survive, THRIVE!

One way to see if you are living in alignment with your gift is to look at your life: is it easy, do you have an abundance of happiness, do your dreams manifest easily? Or do you struggle to make ends meet; do you feel overwhelmed by the amount of energy it takes just to survive? Is happiness something you experience on rare occasions and seems to disappear quickly? Or are you happy most of the time? Do you love the work you do or does your job suck the life out of you?

Universe's Insight: "If you are not using your gifts, you will live in a constant state of failure and struggle because you're not doing what you are here to do. Life is

like a secret mission that you've been sent on, and your gifts are your superpowers.

What is your gift? A gift can be anything. Some people are gifted at music, art, talking, helping, business, sports, food, sex, listening to animals, cleaning, laughing, dancing, healing, marketing, parenting, fishing, yoga, loving, numbers, science—the list is infinite. Nobody else has the exact same gifts as you; they may seem similar, but no two people are born with the exact same way of bringing their gifts to the world. You have to see that what you have to offer is a service to others, no matter what it is. If you're doing it, if you're sharing your gifts from the unique perspective that can only come from you, you cannot lose. In fact, when you store your gifts in the closet of your being and let them collect dust, the Universe starts to think, "Maybe we should give this gift to somebody that will use it." That's when you will notice other people doing what you would love to be doing and having what you would like to have.

Some people are afraid of discovering their purpose in life. Sometimes acknowledging your gift and sharing it is a scary thing; in fact, it is probably your gift that scares you the most! Maybe you have avoided your gift for twenty years or more like I did. It might take a huge amount of courage to start living from your source and using your gift, and it might come with ease and grace.

It's really your choice. If you think it to be hard, it will be; if you think it will be easy and fun, then it will be. Commit to using your gift and sharing it with the world! You will be amazed at what will reveal itself to you!

Here are some of the things that you might be telling yourself that hold you back from using your spiritual gift and being successful. Mentally add anything else that comes up for you:

- **I am not good at it**
- **I don't have the money to do it**
- **I don't have the time**
- **Someday**
- **I'm not allowed**
- **I'm an introvert**
- **People won't accept me if I do that**
- **I'm not smart enough**
- **It's a dream, money is to be hard-earned, if it comes easily, it's too good to be true**
- **I need to be in better shape before I can do that**
- **I don't know where to start**
- **I'll never make it**
- **I just do it as a hobby**
- **Nobody will like it**

Once you become aware of the subconscious programming of your mind, you can start to strengthen yourself by choosing replacement thoughts. With repetition and determination, your replacement thoughts will become new habitual thoughts and your life will change because the way you think about things will have changed.

Here are some of the ways that you can practice strengthening your Asking Muscle:

1. Become a bliss seeker.

Look for the opportunities being presented to you in each moment. There are always decisions to make; it's up to you to move toward what will bring you the most happiness. Find what brings you bliss in each moment. When it stops bringing you bliss, change direction and find something new that adds to your enjoyment in the moment.

What you enjoy in this moment might be totally different in the next. Get out of the routine of automatic unconscious choosing: start ordering your eggs as an omelet instead of scrambled, try a different kind of coffee, do something that scares you, see the variety that the Universe is offering to you.

Happiness is your business, so look for the door that has "good time" written on it and keep moving in that direction. You will be overwhelmed by the abundance of fun you can have. Being a bliss seeker is full of surprise, and I for one happen to love surprises.

2. Steer clear of the happiness thief

There are people who are just not that fun to be around—people who seem to steal the joy from everyone around them. When you find yourself around this energy, make the conscious choice to focus somewhere else.

Find something that makes you feel good and focus there. You see, happiness thieves cannot help themselves; their depressing world as experienced through their senses is different than yours.

Your job isn't to fix them, or figure out why they are the way they are; your job is to give them space to be who they are, while choosing to move toward a more 'feel-good' place for yourself. Leave it alone; it's none of your business.

3. Treat yourself

Remove limitations and consequences from your journey. When you want something, if it presents itself to you, treat yourself, have it and enjoy it. Treat yourself to something that you wouldn't normally let yourself have or do. Keep doing that until you get used to the feeling of getting what you want and desire. Then you can start asking for what you want and be strong enough to say yes to it when it comes.

4. Ask for it!

You asked for it, here it is. This is how easily this law works: when you are clear about what you want and ask for it from a conscious place, it will come to you. Be aware of thoughts of self-doubt that creep in from your subconscious mind and create a fuzzy connection. Ask and feel as though what you ask for is possible, and is on its way. Be certain that what you are saying is what you really want, because you're going to get it either way -- hence the saying, "be careful what you ask for." Ask, visualize, and receive. Ask, visualize, and receive. Repeat. This is what is constantly happening anyway, so become conscious and choose what you want to create. Ask with clarity and awareness.

Universe's Insight: "Get out of your way! What are you doing being an obstacle in your life? An unused gift is a waste. I know this might sound harsh, but if you're walking through your life without using your gift, you're taking up precious time and space. Your gift is a part of you because right now, at this time, you are here as a part of this evolution. This is the source of your greatness! Not one person is here without purpose. You are playing a huge part in the evolution of life and you have something huge to offer. Are you willing to play this game? Are you willing to share your spirit? Something great has invested in you to be here now, doing what you were created to do. This is what you signed up for before you were conceived. Trust that you can do it; stop playing small and get the job done! Be you!

Stop being afraid of your greatness. Stand up and make your investor proud, show the Universe that you are

worthy of this gift, that you are willing to take chances. Play the cards that you have been given and use your gift."

If you look back on the last five years of your life, you will see that the choices that you have made, the things that have happened, and the opportunities that have come up have all been an unfolding of things that you have asked for. All of these things have molded you into who you are now. When you feel called to something, listen to the call and see that each call is another step. You don't need to see the top of the staircase; you only need to see the step that is being offered to you right now and take that step. Trust that when you are ready for the next step it will reveal itself. When you are clear about what you want, simply ask for it and it will come. This is where life starts to feel like a big playground. Play, and have fun creating.

"If you can't ask for what you want, you'll never get what you want"

CHAPTER 6 THINK, IMAGINE, AND FEEL

THE SECRET POWER OF MAGNETISM

Imagination is about the power to visualize. When you practice the art of visualization you become a conscious creator. If you can see it in your mind, it's on its way. Using imagination and visualization are part of my daily meditation practice.

Most of the time when I am meditating, I am using this time to create in my mind, visualizing what I want.

I find it particularly helpful to use these techniques before bed so that the pictures and thoughts can marinate in my subconscious overnight. I also love taking a few moments before sleep to say thank you for all the blessings from the day, and the blessings that are on their way.

I like to go through the people that I love and hold a picture of them in my mind and say a little well wish to them. I love you, and I wish you happiness and health.

"When a child has a dream and a parent says, 'It's not financially feasible; you can't make a living at that; don't do it,' we say to the child, run away from home... You must follow your dream. You will never be joyful if you don't. Your dream may change, but you've got to stay after your dreams. You have to."   ~Abraham

Graciously shared from The Daily Law of Attraction Quotes

Abraham-Hicks, © by Esther Hicks, AbrahamHicks.com
(830) 755-2299.

Universe's Insight: "When you become clear about who you are and what you want right now, the energy of what you want aligns with who you are. The Universe starts to conspire, and things will start happening. It will feel like magic. When things are falling apart, you will realize that this is also part of the Alignment. In fact, things are not falling apart; things are actually falling into place. Your life is constantly unfolding, and everything that happens is a part of what you are creating."

Do you realize that all of your thoughts are your reality? Better yet, do you understand what your thoughts are? I know I've said it before, but I personally needed to be constantly reminded of this "wisdom." When you are concentrating on what you don't want, you see more of what you don't want and you *get* more of what you don't want.

Neale Donald Walsh, Author of Conversations with God says, "you get what you think about whether you want it or not." When you have a thought, whether your conscious or not of what that thought is, the Universe conspires to make this thought manifest into reality.

The first step in being unlimited is to realize that everything you have ever thought about is exactly what you have gotten. This is what is happening every moment in the Universe, the turning of your thoughts into reality. Once you realize this, it will change your life forever. You will start to understand why you have the sicknesses that you have, you will understand why people treat you the way they do.

You will understand why things fall apart, why things come together, the people you meet, how you feel, why you're tired, your eating patterns, why you're successful or why you often fail. You will see the formation of your experience of life more clearly once you become aware of the thoughts to which you give your energy.

"Whatever the mind can conceive and believe, it can achieve." ~ Napoleon Hill

You know better than anybody else what your dream is—or have you locked it away? Did you let it go? For me, my dream has been to write a book. I never really enjoyed reading fiction, though, and in school we only read fictional novels. Within the school system I wasn't very inspired, but on my own I loved writing poetry.

I wrote things about myself that scared my mother. But it was real and raw and it had feeling. Whenever I wrote I felt whole. I would sit in my room for hours writing out feelings, emotions, and inner struggles.

I used to say during high school, and even after, that I was going to write a book someday. I would tell people to watch for my book in stores, even if were strangers and had only spent a few minutes together over some profound conversation.

Someday seemed to never come; seventeen years went by, and during that time I became many things: a Pilates teacher, a yoga teacher, a wife, mother, and a waitress—and yet I still had this longing. I didn't fit the regular mother / wife / yogi description. I found any **box** almost unbearable to be put in.

It's amazing how when we give ourselves a label, others expect us to act and live according to that label. I always felt like there was more waiting somewhere for me! And then, one day recently, I started writing again. I loved it! Everything suddenly made sense: the way I live, why I'm the yoga teacher I am, the mother I am, why I love to nap in the day and stay awake all night, the activities I like, the friends I have. It just all made sense; I'm a writer!

The feeling of not belonging and insecurity that followed me like a dark cloud most of my life was because I was trying to fit into the wrong boxes. I was like uncooked spaghetti trying to fit into a soup can, and sure enough I broke a few things trying to fit. Being a writer is something I know—I feel this, know this, with every cell of my body. I can see where I want to go, who I want to meet. I've never felt so sure about anything in my life.

I've wanted to be many things, but being a writer isn't something I want to be, it's something I know I am because it makes me come alive; I'm obsessed with it. I think I could write until my fingers fall off.

It's the best feeling in the world to feel something being channeled through you. Most of the time I don't even know what I've written. When I read it over I think, holy Shit! I'm nothing short of brilliant! I'd never thought that way about myself before, in any way, about anything. Everything always felt like a struggle, trying to be ok at something, find something I could make a living at.

When I can look at something I've done and think that it's brilliant, it feels amazingly good—beyond good. It feels like this is what being alive is about. Not just living. But really being alive with source flowing through me. This is it! It feels so good to know who I am. Thank you! Thank you! Thank you! Being a writer is awesome, in part because it makes me make sense. It's my gift; it's what I must share with you. Thank you for being here and reading this. I hope you get a feel for what it's like to find it: to find your purpose, your gift.

Getting clear on what you really want can be a daunting process. Our minds can be filled with wanting to do what's right, worrying about what others will think, what is healthy, and even what will make our lives more comfortable 50 years from now. Now, as early as 8th grade or even earlier, we are told to start thinking about our future. Me? I prefer the first-grade approach where we are just asked to dream about what we want to be when we grow up.

Do you see and feel the difference here? Although both are a form of living in the future, one has pressure behind it, a pressure filled with all kinds of covert reasons. The other is about daydreaming, and when we daydream we allow our minds to move toward something that feels good, something that we love.

But what would happen if we asked the question to both groups, eighth graders and first graders, what do you love right now? What do you want to do right now? I can only take a guess that the first graders would have all kinds of fun answers (most likely involving things like play and candy). It's also likely that many of the eighth graders wouldn't know how to answer this question. Some might say, "I'd like to be at home watching TV or surfing online."

We have already forgotten how to enjoy ourselves in the present moment by the time we are young teens. Life gets so serious for us so fast, and time really only seems to be moving faster as we evolve. Children are under more pressure earlier and earlier in their lives. The need to be the best is very high.

Imagine that you suck at something you love to do, imagine being pushed to your limits every time you go out to have fun, imagine people laughing at you because you're unique. Maybe somebody called you names and told you that you were a loser. Perhaps you were always chosen last to be on a team. Chances are good that you've experienced this on some level yourself. As we grow and age, and as more people laugh, call us names, and tease us, we start to conform. We want so badly to belong; however, what we're not taught along the way is that everybody feels the same. Leaving us feeling alone.

Imagine if you were taught that you are perfect the way you are, that you don't need anybody's approval, that your being here on this planet at this time is enough. Imagine if there were no expectations, if your need for approval from your parents and friends disappeared. Imagine the freedom to express yourself fully in every way! Imagine being a version of yourself without boundaries, without the many boxes in which you now live.

We've forgotten who we really are.

We've controlled our unacceptable behavior and we've decided to fit in because on some level, this is what our soul craves.

We want to be loved, we want to belong, and we want to be better than everybody else—or at least equally as good. But somewhere along the journey, we forgot how to dream, we forgot who we are, and we forgot how to think about what we want, because we've trained our thoughts to go along with the crowd. We have been trained to want what everybody else wants. We've been trained to do as we're told.

So for starters, assume that you don't even know what you want.

What Is Your Soul's Desire?

Now, because you have continued to read this, it's safe to say that you desire to know more. You are acting from a place of unknowing, but you're excited— excited about your dreams, about getting clear on what you really want, and about starting to live your dreams and share your gifts with the world. And the feeling is also coming from source moving through you, becoming active, and celebrating the waking up of these long lost desires.

To get clear about what it is that you really want answer these questions.

(BE HONEST WITH YOURSELF!)

- Are you happy?

- Do you enjoy the people you spend your time with?

- Is there something missing such that its presence would make a profound difference in the way that you feel and live? What is it?

- Can you take full responsibility for everything in your life you've created, even if you can't understand why?

- How do you really love to spend your time? What do you really love doing for your own enjoyment?

- Are you doing what you're doing to receive approval from others, or do you do it because you want to do it?

I have spent time talking to amazing people (like yourself!), and what I've noticed is that when people begin their journey towards creating a life they dream of, a life different than the life that they are stuck in (the box), there are a few steps that take place.

Enlightenment is one of the first signs. It's worth noting, however, that enlightenment itself isn't a huge thing; it's your natural state! You were born an enlightened being—we all were. We just become so taught, trained, and boxed up that our natural enlightened state becomes inaccessible. There is no need to search for enlightenment because we are already enlightened; we just need to become aware of our expansive self. It's like waking up, a slow rousing of consciousness and awareness.

First you realize that there is more out there, and then you become able to see that you can have whatever you want.

You and many others are waking up to this realization.

Ten years ago, this topic would have been very difficult to bring up, as people just weren't ready to understand their own power. Now everybody is talking about the law of attraction, about alignment, and we are starting to believe that we are worthy of our dreams.

Howard Thurman said it beautifully in his quote, "Don't ask what the world needs. Ask what makes you come alive, and go do it. Because what the world needs is people who have come alive."

You see, when you get clear on what you want, what makes you come alive, you nurture the entire universe because what you are here to do, your unique being-ness in the world, has only this time in space to deliver it; there will never be another person exactly like you in all of time. Follow your dreams and let them lead the way to your freedom.

Let's return to one of my earlier questions to you: what do you want? As material things are what the brain is used to working with, let's start exercising the manifestation muscle here. Visualize your life: do you want a big house or a small house? I still struggle with this question because of the boxes I've been in. We live under an extreme amount of pressure to conserve, to go green, to make the smallest possible imprint as we walk through life. Although I love this planet and want to build a self-sustainable life (because we've been taught that the world is going to end and its resources are running out), I can't help but wonder what it would be like to dream about my dream home without being held back by fear and an overall belief that wanting something grand is selfish and beyond my means.

I wonder what would happen if we asked a child to talk about their dream home! It would have water slides and big fun rooms, even rides.

Michael Jackson had a huge vision of dreams into reality by creating his Neverland Ranch. Now, do you want a big home or a small home?

My answer was both! Yes, I allowed that to be a possibility, and I realized that I would love to have a big home with a pool and a climbing gym, a big kitchen, a cook and a cleaning helper. I would love to drive a sporty convertible along a beach road. I would love a big, warm fireplace and a country yard adorned with beautiful tall trees! That house would be in the countryside, somewhere in California, but I would also love to have a small wood-cabin-like home near a lake (maybe this is why people have cottages). We would have a boat, and I could paint and write and sleep and enjoy the offerings of nature.

I had never thought that having two homes was a possibility. I didn't even know if having one was possible, let alone two that support two different dreams! I believed that I couldn't afford my dreams, as only rich people could afford to live the cottage life! But, the question was why couldn't I have a rich life?

Well, the answer to that is easy: I didn't believe I could! I spent more time thinking about how unlucky I was than on what I desired. You have to get this. In my mind, I was in a different category. I was amongst the 'settling for what I have' category, and this category was very depressing for me because I had big visions that were constantly being criticized—both by myself and by the people I chose to have close to me. These people criticized me as a dreamer, but here's the ticket: I created and placed these people in my life because I wasn't ready to flourish. I needed help to keep me at that level with all of those dreams.

I love the part in the song "Imagine" by John Lennon where he sings, "You may say I'm a dreamer, but I'm not the only one." I felt connected to the message he was giving and I knew that somebody somewhere understood the way I felt. Yes, I am a dreamer, and being a dreamer is the part that I love the most about myself!

I heard the message come through today that said, Yes you do have big dreams, and you have a lot of desires, and things cost a lot of money, so my dear, if you're going to get what you want, you'll have to make a lot of money. Ah-ha, I thought; the money is the easy part.

I just have to stay aligned and clear about what I want, and the Universe will figure out how to create the opportunity for money to flow.

I like nice things. I love my son, and he loves nice things. I want to see the world, but I don't want to carry a 60-pound pack on my back. I want to drink cappuccino for breakfast and wine at night. I want to reach into my wallet and give spontaneously to somebody hungry on the street, or even invite him or her out for dinner with me.

I don't want to cook three meals every day and clean up after all of them. I want to dress in a stylish outfit— you know, one of those outfits you see in fashion magazines.

I want to walk into a room where I feel amazing because somebody just did my hair, I had a massage earlier, and my dress fits perfectly. I want my sexy, handsome man to walk up and put his hand around my back supportively as he looks into my eyes with amazement before he kisses my forehead in a way as if to say you are beautiful, the woman of my dreams and I'm so blessed that I have this time with you.

Let's dance. Let's celebrate our success together.

Let's laugh and ponder our deepest dreams and most forbidden desires together.

Let's walk hand-in-hand. Let's sing together. Maybe he'll serenade me with his music as we enjoy a picnic among the trees.

I want my son to grow up understanding the power of his thoughts; I want to be an example to him of how our dreams are reachable. I want him to have the most fun in this life! Unlimited fun!

When you start to dream and allow yourself time to fantasize, you begin to feel the emotions that they evoke in you. When you start to believe that you are worthy of your dreams and desires, then they will start to manifest them. Write about what you want, talk about what you want, and notice the signs that the universe is trying to make your dreams come true. SAY YES! Be the creator, and watch it all unfold in ecstasy at your feet

Believe in Yourself

Imagine your dreams coming true. Daydream periodically throughout the day about how you want things to go. Visualize yourself as successfully accomplishing these dreams and desires, and allow these visions to arouse your senses. See things in your mind's eye with the same certainty as you would if it were actually happening.

I once read that when you feel good, you're feeling God. I'm reluctant to use the term God because it stirs up so many emotions for people. But if there is a force that flows through you and me and all things, it doesn't matter whether you call that force Universe, God, Energy, or the Divine.

What you do know is how you feel. When you are doing anything that makes you feel good, anything at all, you are connected to this force.

When things don't seem to be working out the way that you like, try changing the way that you think about the situation instead of trying to change the outside circumstances. Look within and start there.

Who Am I?

The greatest question of all time: who am I? Often when pondering this question, we fill up the answer with our qualities, what we do, our work, and all of the things that we have declared ourselves to be. I could answer this question a number of ways:

I have been a mother, a daughter, a wife, a yogi, a writer. I am a hard worker. Some of you would claim to be a vegetarian, a professor, or maybe a model. We start to add what we have and love in there too: I like skiing, running, wine, food, nature. Then we might talk about the things we own, the things we're proud of; maybe you have three cars, homes in the Hamptons.

Before we know it, the description of who we are becomes a kind of resume. In the hopes of winning over the approval of others, we pick out what makes us sound good. Subconsciously, your life becomes not about you, but about satisfying the needs of others and keeping their positive opinion of you.

I am going to tell you something that will change the way you think about yourself and others: you are *not* what you have, like, and do. You are a spiritual being experiencing these things. We have simply forgotten the experience. We have been so conditioned and leashed and boxed-in that when asked, who are you, our answers all sound the same.

So…really, who are you? What is your natural state—that is, what is natural for you? Do you naturally relax, are you active, do you love to read, take pictures, party? Do you even notice what you talk about with others? Trying to find out who you are is like getting to know somebody else. What you need to do is *listen* to who you really are.

If you're unsure of what your dreams are and you feel stuck when thinking about what you want, ask yourself a few questions that might help you rediscover who you were sent here to be:

What activates a deep sense of happiness when you are thinking about, talking about, or doing it?

What type of books and magazines are around your home?

What could you spend hours at without feeling like you are working—something where time just seems to fly by?

What could you spend your whole life doing without being attached to the financial outcome? Your dream, dharma wants to flow through you without attachment.

How can you serve others? Your dharma is always connected to service; what is your message, your part in evolution? How does what you love doing help others?

Imagine and Feel

Create a collage or dream board. When you're creating your dream board, try not to think too much. Create from a place of feeling. When you're looking through magazines and books, choose the things you're drawn to. When it gives you a good feeling, don't question it, just cut it out and paste it in. Do this same thing in life; when you get a good feeling, don't question it, just paste it in. This is your essence connecting to things that allow it to express itself. You don't need to know why; you just need to follow it! Say yes and let it become part of you!

When you know and ask for what you want, prepare for its arrival.

We are now merging into the process of creating an extraordinary life. Now that you understand your thoughts and are exercising your asking/receiving muscles, I must let you in on the next Insight.

Universe's Insight: "When you are asking for something from a place of not having it, you are subconsciously coming from a place of lack. This is the vibration from which you are asking; as such, what you'll actually experience is more situations that prove to you that you don't have it; you will attract more lack.

Instead of asking for what you want, which can lead to a wishy-washy someday dream state (that you don't truly believe you can have, otherwise you would already have it and not be dreaming about it), ask yourself, What am I ready for? This question presents the space to feel what you are aligned with right now. This is important, as the Universe can only give to you that to which you are vibrationally aligned.

What is your vibration? Take a look at your life; it is the manifestation of your vibrational alignment. If you want to experience something different, you must get clear on what you're ready for and focus on matching your vibration to it. There is an abundant Universe out there, a Universe waiting for you to respond so that it can bring to you that with which you are in alignment with. You can't say you want to be a millionaire, then focus on the things that you hate about money and expect that million dollars to appear. If you want to be a millionaire, start acting like one, speaking like one. Walk the walk. Talk the talk. Talk to bankers. If you can't do that—if that's too much work—you might need to rethink your desire. You can't pretend a vibration. It's a feeling. You are your vibration; you will always get more of what you are. Vibration attracts to it that which it is. Like attracts like. One more time, I ask you, what are you ready for?"

Experiment: Be More Then What You Were Built for

Where do your limitations come from? From the same place that your possibilities come from: your beliefs. Believe it or not, your limitations come with the package. They are part of the programming that has become you. You are your programming. If you are a limited person who struggles to see success in your life, chances are good that you were taught that life is a struggle and that money doesn't come easily.

You may also notice that you have surrounded yourself with people who struggle in similar ways and are in similar situations. You do this because this is your comfort zone; this is what you know and what you're comfortable with.

If you are to step out of the boxes of limitation, you are going to have to spend some time reprogramming the way that you think. Think beyond what you know and believe, and be *more* than what you were built for.

Universe's Insight: "You must first realize the power that you possess. If we could fully embrace the creative power within, then there would only be thought and creation. God-like creative forces live in each of us. We have the power to have all of our thoughts manifest into reality. So what is it that gets in your way? Self-doubt. Fear of failure. Lack of outside support? Some of us need cheerleaders to cheer us on, giving us approval for everything that we do. As soon as we truly understand

that we are the creator of our life and always have been, the faster we can become clear on what it is that we would like to create and start creating! Life is an ongoing process. Create, move on, create, move on, create, move on.

Once you start to believe in the power of your thoughts, you will simply start to choose more successful thoughts. Get really clear about what it is that you want to create in your life. Paint a picture in your mind about what this looks like. Maybe it's a relationship you've always dreamed of, a home that you love, a job doing what you are passionate about, financial abundance, even perfect health. Although all of these may spark a fire in the creator within you, choose one that you would like to focus on for now.

Let's say you choose financial abundance. In your mind's eye as you're reading this, think about what financial abundance feels like to you. Paint a picture, even a movie, about what financial abundance means and looks like to you. Let these words sink deeply into your consciousness and subconscious (whether you believe it or not), I am financially abundant; I Am totally taken care of; my family is taken care of; I can do all that I desire to do; I offer help to those in need; I know that money flows to me like water; I am a money magnet, money is attracted to me; I just can't lose; I love to share my success. Take a few minutes to read this over and over, and add anything else that feels supportive and positive.

You may notice another voice taking over the mantra, one that seems to say, I'll never have that much, this is nothing but crap, I don't even like this book, I'm a failure. This is the voice that keeps you from manifesting your dream. We all have this voice. I now refer to this voice as "my resistance" The trick is to notice it, catch it in its track of destruction, acknowledge it, and begin repeating a positive mantra. Try not to get caught up in making it wrong or judging this voice; simply acknowledge it and choose a more helpful thought.

This form of resetting the way you talk to yourself can be extremely effective when dealing with body image and self-compassion as well. Feel the emotions that go along with the picture or movie that you have been creating in your mind. Ask yourself what would that dream bring to you, how would you feel different, what would you do differently, where would you go, which people would you spend your time with? You might realize that the life that you have now and the people you spend your time with wouldn't change that much. Why? Because this is what you are aligned with right now. You might take your friends on a vacation where you party for a couple weeks, but that's probably what you're doing now. Maybe you would relax on a beach with your family, the family who you spend time with now.

Understand what you are aligned with. Money doesn't change your alignment. Also, allow the journey to unfold. If the journey doesn't seem enjoyable, then you are not actually aligned with what you say you want right now. So stop, look at it, and transition into the direction that you think will make you feel better. In the alpha state, you get to make a conscious choice of what you would like to align with."

The Four Stages of Realization:

1. I'm sick of this

2. I don't know what I want

3. I'm ready; I know who I am and what I am being called to do

4. I'm in the flow

What stage are you in? If you're in the first stage, congratulations! You realize that your life isn't in alignment with what you want and who you know you are. You're ready to move in a new direction. This can be a scary stage because your ego and your soul are going to have disputes. Your ego has become very comfortable with the life that you have, even if the quality of that life is less than ideal.

Your ego, like some people, really dislikes change. Your soul has been awakened and is saying, experience more of what you are, let's feel good, let's have abundant happiness and success. The soul is connected to the infinite intelligence that is all around and within us.

The soul is connected to that which flows through you; it wants you to experience ultimate happiness.

The soul says I'm done, I'm sick of this; I know there is more to be experienced. It thrives in positive vibration. There will be challenges when you move from this stage because you are living at a certain comfort level that's...well, comfortable! That's why you stay there. You need to step out of your comfort zone in order to experience something different than what you experience now.

This is an exciting stage to be in because you are waking up to the call. Be patient; just realizing this is a huge step in your evolution. Transformation is starting. Your mind may be very busy and focused on the negative side: I don't have, I don't know what I want, I'm never going to, I'm too old to pursue something new.

This is your resistance sitting in the comfort zone, avoiding change. Your resistance knows that what you focus on grows, so if you're focused on all the reasons you can't change, you'll get more of what you *don't* want. You'll remain comfortable—this is important to your resistance.

Its job is to keep you small. Go to a place where you can focus on what you *do* want. Say to yourself, I want creativity and fun, joy and health, warmth, new beginnings, love, wealth, if let your desires pour out of you; you will receive those things.

Start with what you are grateful for now, as the vibration of gratitude attracts more of that to itself. In this way, you will receive more to be grateful for.

If you are stuck in the second stage—the 'I don't know what I want' stage

You may be trapped in boxes that were developed throughout your life- through other people, media, religion, teachers, even mass consciousness. When we become trapped in boxes, we forget how to listen to our own inner nature. Instead of being a singer, you become a dentist.

 We often lose the senses of creativity and determination that we had as a child. We lose the ability to want with passion and desire because we are told over and over again that we can't do this and we can't do that.

What happens over time is that you believe it. So you went with the boring recommendation of the masses that you should go for whatever will bring you the most money, because the most money—no matter what—will bring you happiness, right? Wrong!

It's the way in which you make your money that will bring you wealth and happiness. You must love what you do. But if you're a dentist who loves to sing, and singing is the only thing that makes you feel alive, and you haven't hummed a note for thirty years, you can have all the money in the world and you're never going to be satisfied.

When you are asked the question, what do you want, what is the first thing that comes to you in this moment? Maybe it's a cup of coffee. Okay, go get a cup of coffee. Then once you have your cup of coffee, ask yourself again, what do I want? Maybe this time it's a hamburger. So, go get a hamburger. Then after you have your hamburger, ask yourself again: what do I want? Maybe this time it's a home, a lover, or maybe to become an artist.

There is no right or wrong; it's just about listening to what you want and believing that you can have it. Notice how what you want is in constant change. Imagine zero limitations, zero consequences, and the amount of money you could make or spend does not matter. Now ask, what do I want? Your answers may feel like they were preprogrammed coming from your subconscious mind. The more you play this game, the more authentic your answers will be, and the more you'll start to remember what it is that you *really* want. Let go of the need to please anybody else with your answers. After all, you are asking yourself what *you* want. If you want to know what your mother wants, go ask her! If you want to know what *you* want, ask yourself!

The third stage is a very magical place to be. If you know who you are, if you feel in touch with your calling and you're ready to roar like a lion, the chances are good that you have been through the last two stages and you are experiencing the freedom of *being alive*.

The Universe is opening itself up to you; opportunities are abundant and seem to be jumping out at you.

In this stage of realization you have burst through the boundaries where your beliefs had confined you. Your boxes don't exist anymore, and you feel free. You're in the 'anything is possible' stage. You are ready, you know who you are, and what you're being called to do.

You are confident, and you have a glow around you to which other people are attracted. Sometimes in this stage, old ways of being and thinking can creep up on you; however, you recognize them right away because they don't feel good. You have experienced what freedom feels like, and those old ways of being just don't serve you anymore.

We could also call this stage the 'yes' stage, because you are ready to say yes to life—you are back on the path you used to enter this life. You know who you are. An important thing to remember in this stage is to be mindful of resistance when it creeps up.

The fourth stage is when you have realized your power; you move through your life effortlessly and the Universe delivers what you need when you need it. It seems as though things are always happening perfectly in this stage. You are riding the wave, enjoying each unfolding, where each experience is part of the evolving process. You seem to understand the connection between all things. You are clear and consciously choosing your life.

This stage offers itself to you as you become clear about who you are. When you connect to your soul and begin nurturing its needs—when you are in the flow—you own your world. Nobody and nothing can take your happiness from you because it comes from a deep place of inner satisfaction and connection. You always seem to be in the right place at the right time. New ideas and inspirations come to you constantly and without effort. In this stage you are limitless. You are *unstoppable*.

Albert Einstein said, "Imagination is more important than knowledge." In Ziggy Marley's song, "Love is My Religion," he sings about wisdom as "not in the books do I find, but by searching my mind." I don't know about you but I can certainly feel the difference between somebody who has studied a book about religion and somebody who knows divine love through experience—simply take a look at historical examples like Buddha and Mother Theresa.

Daydream

Before bed one night my son said to me, "I want to have a mansion." I curiously asked him "why." He responded with an extremely excited, "Because it would be awesome! I could have my own science lab, a theatre, a pool, and I could walk to the beach!" This kid was talking my language! So I pulled up California mansions on the computer, and of course he wanted to look at the most expensive ones, so we looked at pictures of homes spanning from thirty million dollars all the way down to a measly ten million. I swear, some of these homes were bigger than the town I live in. One even had a heart- shaped pool! I had so much fun dreaming with him. I always do! Want to expand your mind? Spend some time with a young person and talk about your dreams!

Let Yourself Dream

Let yourself dream about what you want. Make time each day to visualize how you want it to go. How do you want your life to feel?

Athletes do this in competitions all the time, and a lot of athletes who reach the top of their sport use these visualization techniques. Treat your life as though you were a top competitor. Play on the field, and practice. Exercise the right muscles, and focus daily on your dreams.

If you desire to manifest things with your mind but spend no time thinking about them and visualizing them, and instead go to the gym and exercise and obsess about your abs, you will acquire great abs; however, the other parts of your dream will disappear into the background.

If you want great abs but don't go to the gym all the time, and instead spend your time mentally, consciously thinking about great abs, you will still get great abs. Your visual and mental determination, followed by action, can create miracles faster than just doing because there is clarity, feeling, and imagination involved.

The "Everythingist"

Before bed one night I asked my son what he would like to be in twenty years—where he would like to live, who he would be, what would he see? He thought for a moment or two and looked up into infinity and responded quickly with a brilliant answer. He said, "I will be an everythingist!"

"An everythingist, "I replied, "Well, that's brilliant, I want to be an everythingist too!" We laughed for a few minutes in a basking-in-the-brilliance kind of way, like two witches that had just created a new love potion, laughing out loud from the bottom of our guts.

I have been playing with this context for a week, and tonight I was telling a colleague at work about the everythingist conversation. My coworker said to me, "Would you rather master something or be an everythingist?" My answer was an immediate *everythingist*. I have no ambition to be a master at something. I do not strive to compete to be the best; I just want to dip my fingers in as much as possible while I am here on this beautiful Earth. This life is a gift—I want to experience it all! For some of you, mastering something is what you crave.

There may be times in your life where you feel that mastering something is your mission, and at other times you want to be free and ride the wave of everythingism. Trust that your guidance is on track. You have the ability to make choices and change direction whenever you please. After all, we are all masters at life. Remember, you are continuously creating the life you live! So right now in your life, do you want to master something, or be an everythingist? Both are amazing ways to live, and realizing that the choice is yours is very powerful!

Universe's Insight: When you pretend, you actually activate pathways in the brain that free up your imagination. Picture yourself sailing on the ocean, or pretend to be on a talk show on TV; imagine you're a great lover, or pretend to be an amazing artist; maybe dress up and imagine yourself as a millionaire. Your cellular body doesn't know the difference between your 'reality' and when you're pretending, so when you're pretending, a deep inner part of you actually believes it's real. The more you pretend, the more you believe it to be. This is really another way of saying visualize what you want or your thoughts become your reality.

Accept that when you pretend, you put more than just your mind into it. As a child you loved pretending; find the part of yourself that is playful and unattached to the

outcome. Have fun pretending. Life is your stage; indeed, most of the time you're acting anyway. Treat yourself and spend some time immersed in some scheduled pretend time. Maybe even invite your closest friends in on a special pretend evening. Maybe you all act like famous people, T.V show hosts, healers, porn stars, whatever you want! The intention is to have fun and play the part of the person you see yourself becoming. Not only will you surprise yourself by how much fun you will have, but you might notice that the Universe also plays right along with you.

"Think it, Feel it, Imagine it!"

CHAPTER 7 CREATE AND JUMP

JUMP INTO THE UNKNOWN WITH DRUNKEN ABANDON... I'LL CATCH YOU! ~UNIVERSE

There is something extraordinary about your mind. Have you ever stopped to notice the amount of information that you download every second? Besides your thoughts and ability to learn, your brain is constantly working to make your world make sense to you. Everything you see is being downloaded and judged so that you can have an understanding of what your external environment is. The only thing is, what you see is not actually the way things are!

Look around you right now and take in all that's there: the colors, the names you give things, your likes and dislikes, what you believe to know about things. Now bring your other senses into this game. What do you hear, smell, taste, and touch? What are the thoughts and judgments around the information that your senses are sending your brain?

Although your brain has an unlimited amount of information coming in at a constant speed, you are able to live in this world of abundant information because your brain categorizes everything and gives things a name so that you have this feeling of knowing.

When you feel that you know something, you stop questioning it. As a result, you walk through life on autopilot and become unaware of what is really happening around you.

Everything in the Universe is vibrating at different frequencies: your TV, your home, the stuff in your home, your pets, your car, your water…you get the point. Why can't you see this vibration? The answer is simple, and you might not like it. Your world is understood by how your brain has been programmed. If you and I were to sit and look at the same tree at the same time, we would both experience the tree differently.

We can't see the vibration at which things are moving because we have been taught what they are—and we look no further. I don't expect that people will start to see vibration; instead, what I intend is to open a new window of your mind so that you can experience things from unknowing. My goal is to help your untaught, un-programmed mind once again experience life as a mysterious unfolding. Let life teach you; it is time to let go of what you believe to be true.

Having powerful thoughts without taking action when opportunities come is like planting a vegetable garden and never giving it water. Your vegetables will never grow; instead, they will remain as seeds in the ground, waiting. In this same way your thoughts remain thoughts when action isn't taken. You can think and think and think that you're going to be a singer, but when somebody asks you to sing at a party you say no. And when you see a flyer on the street advertising singing lessons, you think to yourself, I don't have the money to pay for singing lessons.

Although your soul is being pulled to these things, you stay small; you say no to the calling. You don't even let yourself sing in the shower because you're afraid somebody might hear you! Does this sound like the way a winner wins? Are you up for the challenge, ready to jump?

One of the things we have forgotten is the power of our imagination! When you spend time dreaming and visualizing, you activate a power far greater than your mind can grasp.

You create things into being every time you think, imagine, and speak. Don't you think it might be beneficial to choose the things that you activate rather than letting other forces choose these things for you? If you want to be rich but are caught in the thought of a bad economy; that the rich get richer and the poor get poorer (and you're in the poor group) you will be relegated to envying the rich. Oh, and guess who stays poor and gets poorer?

That's right, you! If you choose thoughts of wealth and prosperity and opportunity, then you will receive opportunities that bring you prosperity and wealth. And you will be among the rich.

The reason that you are reading this book is to bring into your life a sense of imagination and power. I want you to step away from what you have been attached to and start living your dreams. Stop being depressed/suppressed and get clear on what you want so you are able to hold a vision of it.

Let the power of the Universe bring it to you this way, keep visualizing it, then get out of the way—let go of the need to supervise.

Trust that each opportunity will be given to you at the perfect time, and act on these opportunities as they come. Let's dive into the world of infinite possibility and find what it is that makes you come alive.

Universe's Insight: In order to understand the concept of infinite possibilities, you must understand the concept of infinity. It is never-ending; there is always more. It is vast and boundless. Immeasurable, fathomless. You see, your problem is that you can't understand infinity without experiencing how immense infinity really is. You are somehow looking for a way to explain it.

This is like someone trying to explain God, or love: you can never explain or fully understand it because as soon as you put words to it, you lose the essence of its never-ending nature. You are also infinite. The only reason you can't access your unlimited nature is because you have been programmed to believe that you are not. As soon as you access your infinite potential, you will see that you can have anything that you vibrationally match up to. You are what you are, you have what you are. If you want something different, you will have to change your vibration.

What I've noticed when talking to people about what they want, and what they love to do, is that a number of things happen in this conversation:

People are scared to talk about what they want because they fear that sharing their dream will sound silly and irresponsible.

People talk about their dreams as if those dreams were merely an unrealistic hope.

People start to light up after a few minutes as their dream becomes possible in their own mind, inspiring those who are listening.

A big, contagious smile appears, illuminating these people from the inside out; their whole energy changes when they take their power back.

I am available for private coaching and spiritual gift retrieval. If you're interested in diving deeper into your fullness, you can contact me through my www.astralily.com website. You can start taking the first steps toward living a more purposeful life today. I can't wait to see you light up!

Universe's Insight: "When a baby bird takes its first steps towards the end of the branch and jumps for the first time, it has no idea what could happen. It is leaving its nest, the place that has been its nurturing home for so long, surrounded by comfort, warmth and family. In a human life, this place that you create—your home, your

way of living—becomes comfortable. And while living a comfortable life for some is fine, some of you crave to know what else is waiting beyond your comfort zone. The thing is, you don't know what is waiting for you until you jump!"

Brain Frequency

I have found it extremely helpful and intriguing to learn about the different frequencies of the brain, and have learned to use them to benefit my life as I consciously create it. It has made such a significant difference that I would be shortchanging you if I didn't share this magic!

Your brain activity can be measured, actually, the speed at which the neurons of the brain communicate. The frequency or brain wave activity relates to the speed of this neurological communication; picture sound waves bouncing back and forth. This brain wave activity is measured in Hertz, abbreviated as Hz. Scientists and doctors can actually measure your brain wave activity by hooking you up to an EEG (electroencephalogram).

Brain wave frequency has been grouped by speed into four main groups:

Beta 14-30Hz—Highly Alert

Alpha 8Hz-14Hz—Relaxed but alert - Still in control of thoughts

Theta 4Hz-8Hz—Drowsy (also the first stage of sleep)

Delta 0.5Hz-4Hz—Deep sleep

There are other types of brain frequency, but our focus will stay on these four main groups.

Beta 14-30 Hz is the frequency that most of us function at when we are awake, when we are working and playing and focused on the external world. Getting tasks done and running your daily life is done at a state of Beta for most people. I think of Beta frequency as a kind of autopilot: you are not necessarily consciously aware of what you are doing. Although things tend to get done at the Beta state, you don't pay attention to your thoughts and feelings at this frequency.

The higher the frequency while at Beta, the more confusing and unfocused your energy will be. If you don't take breaks from the Beta state you will most certainly - burn out!

On the positive side, Beta frequency is a frequency that has a lot of movement and action, so if you need to get things done on the physical plane, this is the frequency to tap into. When I am in need of some Beta energy, I do something that gets me moving. When your body moves faster, your heart rate speeds up, which also serves to activate a faster frequency in the brain.

Alpha 8-14 Hz frequency is my favorite frequency in which to create. When you relax and start to listen to your thoughts, the mind slows down—*everything* starts to slow down. We have this idea in the West that slowing down isn't a good thing, something that shouldn't be done until you retire. We actually schedule our lives so that we know when we will be able to relax. Most of you have scheduled that time to start when you are around the age of 65.

I take daily doses of relaxation; if there is one thing I'm very good at, it would be relaxing. I'm not one to wait 30-40 years to enjoy some 'me' time. But what I have found is that it is very easy for me to go from relaxed in the Alpha state to Theta, which is a drowsy state, and then quickly to Delta; before I know it, I've gone from a little relaxation to a deep sleep. Not that there is anything wrong with a little nap time, but when I want to access the conscious creation of my life, I want to sustain an Alpha state, and here is why: when you lower the frequency of the brain to the Alpha state, you can focus more. When you pair up this super focus with a meditational state, you can create your life, as you want it to be. Sounds too good to be true, I know, but trust me; it is amazing.

Going into the Alpha State is an amazing journey. It's a meditative state where you are consciously aware of your thoughts. It's possible to create at this frequency because of the antennae-like connection to the Universe that is accessed. In the Alpha state you will often receive clear instructions, insights, and visions from the Universe. I think any guided meditation is done at Alpha if you are immersed into the thoughts and visions that you are having.

The powerful part about creating and visualizing at this state is that your connection to the Universe is very strong. Because you are aware of what you are creating, you can direct how you want it to go. In my first Alpha state meditation, I visualized myself at a book signing. I was able to experience the feelings as though it were really happening. When I finished my meditation, I sat down at my computer and wrote all night long.

My fingers were moving so fast that I couldn't even make sense of what I was writing.

When I woke up the next day, I read what I had written and couldn't believe what was on the page. I knew that there was a powerful force that I had connected with; it was the words of the Universe being expressed through my fingers. I cried. I felt whole and complete. I now create my life by going into an Alpha state meditation—it's like visualizing your dreams into reality! Could it be this easy? I know it is, because what I visualize comes to be.

Access your superstar mind. Alpha is a frequency at which superstars function at on a regular basis. Something like four percent of humans naturally function at the Alpha state most of the time, and the other 96 percent function primarily at the Beta state. I recommend doing some research in this area if it calls to you! It is fascinating.

Have you ever wondered why some people seem to make their dreams come true almost overnight, then another dream, and another and another? Look at Oprah, Madonna, Michael Jackson. I even have a couple of friends that seem to make things happen magically in their life with little or no effort at all. Do you know people in your life like this? They just seem to have it all; it's like their Manifestation Muscle is super strong.

Well, my theory is that these people naturally spend more time with their brain functioning at the Alpha Level. They think it; they visualize it, and boom! It happens. If you struggle to make things happen in your life, pay attention to your thoughts and your visualizations, take some time to meditate, and visualize yourself being successful at what it is you want. I swear by this technique. Before you know it, you'll be looking at your life thinking, Wow, did I do that? Look at what I've created! I'm a freakin' superstar!!! Whoop Whoop!

Theta 4-8 Hz is the drifting stage. In this stage, you start to become unconscious of your thoughts and the world around you. Theta is the frequency of the brain that is accessed during the first stage of sleep. This seems to be a hard frequency for a lot of people to readily access. People who have trouble sleeping are often going to bed while their brain is still functioning at a Beta level. This is what is happening when you hear people talking about how they couldn't sleep because there was too much going through their minds.

Yes, the mind is a very busy place! And if we have no training on how to slow these fast moving, often repetitive thoughts down, we are left with an uncontrolled monkey mind. When we are able to slow this frequency down, the parasympathetic nervous system kicks in and starts releasing these yummy, relaxing chemicals into the body, and we are able to relax deeply and fall sleep.

If somebody is constantly in need of a substance to help them fall asleep, it could be that they are unable to easily go from the high vibration of the Beta state to the Theta state; they need help to slow down the monkey mind. For some, the Theta state is like a drug; it is a very easy way to numb themselves from what is happening in their lives.

Chronic fatigue, depression, and chronic sickness all seem to be places where people go to numb themselves against what's really happening. For some it is easier to be unconscious in their lives. When accessed in a balanced way, the Theta state can bring balance to your life as it restores the body and mind from the busy-ness of life and the constant chatter of the monkey mind.

Delta 0.5-4Hz is the frequency that the brain activates during deep, dreamless sleep. At this frequency you are not connected to this world as you know it. Instead, there is a connection to all with no judgments where unconscious oneness is experienced. This is the state of 'I am. I am all that is.'

I think that many people outsource Delta states through drugs and alcohol. All we really want is to feel connected and like we belong. When people intoxicate themselves with stimulants to a point where they pass out, Unconscious Bliss is what they are seeking. If only for a moment or two, they can experience this deep state of nothing—the empty space where love, belonging, connection, and oneness is experience. For me, the Delta state is a non- physical world where all that is, is. Did I mention how much I love sleeping?

At What Brain Frequency Do You Naturally Vibrate?

It is important to understand your natural brain frequency. Once you understand your natural vibrations, you can work on the states that will bring balance to your life. If you have trouble sleeping, you might want to work on activating the frequencies of Theta and Delta. If you sleep too much, are lethargic, and find it hard to complete tasks, you might want to work on activating the Beta waves. If you would like to find out which frequency might be predominantly running your life and find balance for optimizing your manifestation potential, take this short quiz.

Brain Frequency Quiz:

When you go to bed you,

A. Sleep very well and don't need a lot; 5-6 hours a night is good for you

B. Always have trouble sleeping, toss and turn all night, your mind is very active

T. Dream a lot and need a lot of sleep because you don't sleep very deeply

D. Love to sleep; you could stay in bed and drift in and out of sleep all day

When you are awake you,

A. Are focused, take adequate breaks, and overall feel a sense of peace and gratitude

B. Feel energized, accomplish a lot, and don't stop to relax throughout the day

T. Find it hard to stay focused throughout the day and become sleepy often

D. Feel tired most of the time

When was the last time you spent twenty minutes in meditation?

A. Within the last 24 hours

B. Never

T. I Meditate daily, but often fall asleep during my meditation

 D. I would rather sleep then meditate

How easily do you become angry?

A. I don't really get angry; I just walk away from situations that bother me

B. I am constantly rushed, road raged, and angry at somebody

T. I numb myself from anger by taking a happy/relaxing stimulant such as alcohol, marijuana, antidepressants etc.

 D. I sleep it off

Your friends would say that you're

A. Fun, relaxed, and calming to be around; you see the greatness in all

B. High-strung, fast moving, talks a lot, and are confusing at times

T. Out there, flakey, not really connected to reality

D. A loner, susceptible to addictions, depressed

What kind of work do you enjoy doing?

A. Relaxed but stimulating

B. Fast-moving and in control

T. Computer/ office work

 D. I do not like work at all

On average you feel mentally

A. Clear

B. Crazy

T. Slow

D. Numb

In your spare time, you,

A. Daydream

B. Work/Work Out

T. Relax

D. Sleep

When a stressful situation presents itself to you,

A. Breathe deeply and look at different perspectives

B. Freak out, get mad, and feel out of control

T. Have a drink (alcoholic beverage)

D. Sleep it off

What type of books do you enjoy reading?

A. Inspirational life changing books, mostly non-fiction

B. Textbooks and Horror/suspense/mystery/fiction

T. Magazines

D. I hate reading, it puts me to sleep

What is your favorite activity?

A. Yoga and light relaxing movement such as Qigong

B. Competitive fast-moving sports, running, hockey, skiing,

T. Light walking

D. Hot baths and deep sleeps

How do you view the world?

A. I consciously choose my life; I am always in the right place at the right time

B. Stressful and out of control

T. I'm bored and want some excitement in my life

D. I feel like the world owes me something; things just don't work out for me.

When you answer the questions above, do you end up with mostly A's B's D's or T's

A's = Alpha

B's = Beta

D's = Delta

T's = Theta

It is important to be able to access all of these brain frequencies so that you can bring balance into your life—so that you can sleep well, work efficiently and play hard when you want to, connect to the insights from the Universe, and listen to your own inner wisdom and so that you can understand the subconscious mind via your dreams. We really don't want to stay in one frequency all the time.

We are diverse beings, and it is nice to "switch it up" so that we can use more of our brains to manifest the life we dream of. With focus, concentration, and practice, we can help our brains achieve the different frequency states. Accessing all the different frequencies helps us achieve balance and allows us to be more effective in our daily actions, whether that means better sleep, higher energy, connecting with the

Universe, or truly listening to your own thoughts. The exercises that follow will help you access the different frequency states to be able to tap into your brain's full potential.

Become Active at the Beta State

Even if you strongly dislike being active, find ten to twenty minutes each day where you are dedicated to a fast-moving activity. Become strongly aware of your five senses and how they experience the world around you. Open the windows and let the fresh air invigorate you. Do some math or problem solving.

Drive down a busy city street. What you are doing is stimulating a faster frequency of the brain, so do something fast. Even talking fast to a friend can help (though you should probably explain what you are doing first!) Beta frequency is generally associated with the left brain, the literal, mathematical, fast-paced side of the brain.

Fast activity isn't the only way; you can also access the left side of the brain using this stimulation breathing exercise.

Right Nostril Breathing to Access the Left Brain

Sit in a relaxed position. Take the left hand up to the left side of your nose and plug the left nostril with the left thumb. Breathe only through the right nostril, inhaling and exhaling with long, slow, deep breaths. Do this breathing exercise for up to five minutes to activate the left brain and Beta frequency.

Easily Tune Into Your Success at Alpha -- A Meditation

Sit in a comfortable position. If you lie down, you risk becoming drowsy and falling asleep. This is a relaxed but alert state. Close your eyes and gaze upward toward the third eye point (between the eyebrows.) Take five deep breaths, focusing on the flow of breath and how it moves through you. Now visualize yourself looking out into an infinite number of bubble Universes. Each one of your dreams from the past and present has come true in one of these bubbles.

Let's say when you were twelve that you wanted to be an artist; now, see the bubble where you became a talented and successful artist, the bubble where you became a singer, the bubble where you meet your lover, the bubble where you are a millionaire, and so on. Some scientists believe that for each thought you have, an alternate Universe is created, and this thought or dream happens and manifests fully in another Universe. See all of your thoughts and dreams manifested and happening in their own little bubble Universe.

Now, with the keen vision of your third eye, choose which Universe you would like to visit. For example, if you would really like to be a musician, find that Universe and connect to it. Then jump! Jump into this bubble Universe and see yourself as a very successful musician. Take in all that you can; observe how you, as a musician, act, what you're wearing, the people you're with. Take in all the details from all of your senses: smell, sound, intuitive feelings. Really take your time watching yourself being successful. Know that it's you.

Now go up to your twin self (the You in the new Universe you are visiting) and start asking yourself questions that you might have. How do I do it? What should I do next? Whatever questions jump out at you. Listen deeply to the answers. Often in these Alpha meditations, I am told in detail what to do. I've been told who to call, what clothes to wear, how to write -- all kinds of information. When you've finished the Q&A, thank your twin self; feel the gratitude and mean it.

Then jump back into your awareness in this physical world, take a few deep breaths, and integrate what you have learned. If you need to, write any notes down for reminders. The Universe will start bringing you opportunities. And when these opportunities are given to you, it is your responsibility to take action.

Activate the Theta State: 20 Breaths Technique

Lie down and cover yourself with a warm blanket. Make yourself so comfortable that you feel like melting butter. Keep making any physical adjustments to your body; add pillows under the knees, adjust anything you need to create a deep state of relaxation. Begin taking long, deep breaths, starting at twenty. With each breath, slowly count your way down to zero. A complete breath is one full inhalation and one full exhalation. For example, on your first inhalation you would mentally say twenty and on your first exhalation you would also mentally vibrate twenty. Then you would inhale and exhale the number nineteen, then eighteen, and so on all the way down to zero. If you lose track along the way, start back at twenty.

Trust me, by the time you get to zero; you will be so relaxed that you will be drifting off to dreamland. On the rare occasions I have breathed my way to zero and still felt too stimulated to sleep, I simply start the twenty breaths technique again. I have never had to do it three times. Enjoy drifting into relaxed states of sleep; you are worthy of relaxing deeply.

Deep Sleep Delta Method -- Left Nostril Breathing to Access the Right Brain

Delta is really a deeper state of the Theta frequency. You can easily drift from Theta to Delta using the twenty breaths technique described above. But before you begin the twenty breaths technique, do left nostril breathing for up to five minutes. You can do left nostril breathing while you are lying down and completely comfortable according to the guidelines for the Theta state above.

Take your right hand up to the right nostril and plug off the right nostril using your right thumb. Inhale and exhale through the left nostril only. This activates the relaxed, parasympathetic side of the right brain. These techniques together will have you drifting off into a deep, deep sleep so that when you wake up, you will be feeling well rested and ready to take on the world.

Using your results from the questionnaire, create balance in your life and use your brain to its full potential. If you have lots of energy but seem to be unable to manifest things, practice going to the Alpha state daily. If you are tired all the time, you may need to activate the Beta frequency so that you can act on things that you ask for.

Perhaps you're not sleeping deeply at night and this is zapping your energy. If your mind seems busy at night, you could benefit from activating the Theta state. You are the only one who really knows yourself. If you really want to use more of your brain to activate your full potential, you will need to be honest and put the discipline into creating time for these balancing techniques. This will permit you to move through life with the confidence that comes from knowing that you can have and do anything that you put your mind to.

Starting from here, if you had the ability to do be and have anything, who would you be? What would you have, and what would you be doing ten years from now?

Do you believe that you can accomplish this? Can you be unattached to the outcome?

What I've learned is that anything is possible when you believe it to be. It doesn't really matter if it can be proven; the experience of it working is enough!

Universe's Insight: "What you visualize, you become. Become aware of what you spend your time visualizing, what you watch on TV, what pictures does the music you listen to put in your mind, what books do you read, what people inspire you, who do you spend your time with. You'll begin to notice that what you see, you become. That means that what you see happening around you, you become. The thoughts that you have about the things that you experience in your life become your reality.

You and your partner may live in the same home, eat the same food, raise the same children; yet, you have two completely different visions of reality. Come to the realization that you create your reality. Become the hawk watching your thoughts and observing how you speak to yourself. Realize what your visions are. Spend time getting to know what you are thinking, what your subconscious thoughts are. Pay attention to each word.

What does the background music of your mind sound like? Be honest, and evaluate your life. You will see that you have gotten pretty much what you have envisioned for yourself. Pay special attention to your thoughts that are focused on what you *don't* want, as you've learned, they don't work the way that you think. If your thoughts

are in the form of I don't want to struggle, I don't want to drink anymore, I don't want to be poor, these sneaky thoughts are designed to make you believe that you're on the right track.

Unfortunately, these are very limiting thoughts; as such, you will inevitably create situations that cause more 'not wanting to struggle', and more 'not wanting to drink', more 'not wanting to be poor'...do you get it? What you focus on, you will receive. So the real key in manifesting your dreams is to become aware of the context of your subconscious and conscious thoughts. Then, armed with this awareness, consciously choose the thought that you want to manifest."

Beyond Brain Frequency

In the realm that is dream manifestation; three kinds of people exist: Thinkers, Imaginative Action Takers, and Non-Imaginers.

Thinkers are people who are all talk and no action, and you will observe that these people are very good at what they do. They spend hours and hours daydreaming and talking about ideas or get-rich-quick schemes, but nothing seems to change for them. Thinkers tend to always have the same money problems, the same relationship issues; the seeds of their ideas and daydreams never have a chance to sprout! We can think of this state of being as vision without action.

Imaginative Action Takers are the people that we notice in our lives and in the world— the man who seems to effortlessly buy up property in a small town as if he's playing a giant Monopoly game. The Madonnas and Donald Trumps and Wayne Dyers. It's not that these people necessarily started out with more opportunity; the only thing different is that when they have a vision, they act on it. They believe in their vision and they follow it through. They don't sit around waiting for something to happen; instead, they find opportunity and jump on it. These people, these Imaginative Action Takers, are constantly in action.

Non-Imaginers are people who feel stuck, like life has happened to them and they have nothing to do with the results. These people do not aspire to do anything; they have no drive and are typically quite dull and often depressed. The world seems black and white to Non-Imaginers. They often call themselves realists, and the world seems like a bad place to them.

Universe's Insight: Become aware of how many realizations, ideas, and inspiring thoughts you have every day! Write them down. As you do, you will start to see who you are, the things you enjoy, music you like, speakers and quotes that empower you.

These are the things that attract you, and these are the things that you attract to yourself. These things are like clues to understanding your true nature. Say to yourself, I am ready to tune into the potential of this human mind.

It is my connection to the Universe. It attracts things to me like a magnet; this I know. I experience success in my life when I visualize at the Alpha State. With the balanced action taken from my Beta State, I know there is nothing I can't do.

A Little Bit About My Journey

Before understanding my part in creating my own existence, my life was pretty average. Having an average life was all I had ever known. I didn't grow up around people who talked about dreams, and I never really felt a desire for anything. As I saw it, life was about hard work and struggling to get by. I didn't know anything else. So when I watched *The Secret* in my early twenties, something woke up inside me and said, "What the hell are you doing!?"

Of course, there was this other voice that said, "It can't possibly be that simple." This event in my life was a turning point—a time when I started listening to my thoughts. I understood why I had the life I had and I thought, hmm, well it's worth a try! People started talking about *The Secret* and manifestation, and I felt drawn to the people who believed this theory that what you think about, you become.

I began to put the theory to work. I started saying yes to things that I desired instead of brushing them under the carpet of my humdrum life! I saw the light, you might say, and the only way to describe it is to say that it felt good. Even if it didn't work every time, I felt empowered, alive for the first time. Little did I know that what was happening was the biggest gift: it was the golden ticket! I started realizing my dreams. I could hear the thoughts that kept holding me back, the thoughts that diminished me.

I started testing this theory, and when I became aware of the thoughts that held me back and lowered my self-esteem, I made a conscious effort to replace them with those that were more aligned with what I wanted to create. I am a completely different person now.

I am completely different because of the effort I put into changing my thought patterns. Before, I was completely unaware of the thoughts I was having; however, when I became aware, I understood why I had what I had, why I was what I was, and why I felt the way I felt.

I was completely limited and I didn't even know it. The one thing you should note about reading this book is that it will change your life. Are you ready for that?

CHAPTER 8 ACT

IT'S TIME TO TAKE ACTION AND START THE MOMENTUM

"We should be taught not to wait for inspiration to start a thing. Action always generates inspiration. Inspiration seldom generates action."

- Frank Tibolt

Action doesn't mean just physical activity. I like how Benjamin Franklin put it: "Never confuse motion with action." When you are in action, things keep coming. When you start the momentum of a goal, the Universe starts flowing—and the Universe likes speed!

When you get clear on what it is that you want and you ask for it. Immediately go to the Alpha State and start meditating on the successful outcome of your dreams.

When you start to feel and experience yourself as the person about whom you dream of being—once you *believe* it—you will see it!

So you had better be ready when you start seeing the signs, as the world will open up doors for you that you didn't even see before. You will be asked to go places that scare you, and all of your excuses will begin to sweep through your mind: I don't have the money, the support, I need help, my body, blah blah blah...the mind likes the state where you are.

You like this state where you are. Otherwise, you wouldn't be here.

Acknowledge where you are, be grateful, and let your mind know that you are going for it and that it is safe. It'll work out better than you could have ever imagined!

It's time to take action. See the opportunities being given to you and jump on them; if you start saying no and turning away from them, you are closing the door, and the Universe will understand that you don't want the things that you asked for. Your message becomes fuzzy and confusing, and the channel becomes unclear. When you ask, you must act. I say it again: the Universe likes speed!

Keep Up! We all know from experiencing this life that time goes by quickly. There are times when weeks seem to go by in only a fraction of the time and, even though it seems like you just put them away, you're unpacking Christmas decorations again.

When you ask, you must know that you will be asked in turn to do things. There will be challenges and pressure; you don't get somewhere without strength, determination, and keeping up with what is being asked.

Think of the way a seed sprouts: at first, the sprout needs water and sunshine (a little love and encouragement helps too). It has to dig through the grit to follow the warmth and light. The little seedling doesn't give up.

It is part of nature. The seedling doesn't question its quest, it just knows. This is the knowing you must feel and develop within.

Let your success flow to and through you. Believe that it all comes at the perfect time, that there is no need to rush. Be a part of nature and believe that your dream is your destiny; just as it is the seedling's destiny to grow into a majestic tree, it is your destiny to be that what you so deeply—and too often secretly— desire.

Universe's Insight: "If you have a goal, you will think about it and you will talk about it; but if you want it to come to be, you must take action toward it. If you do not, your goal stays afloat in the world of thought. Action is the chemical reaction for manifestation to take place. If you really want to accomplish something, ACT."

Get your groove on.

I know you have a lot of things to do in your day? Make meals, pay bills, call family, work, clean the house, do taxes...this list could go on for a very long time. Truth be told, I could probably write a book called *The Things Humans Do Every Day to Stay Busy*. But what I want to emphasize here are those items that take up space in our minds and in the thought vortex. When we let this build up with undone to-do lists and unfinished projects, the channel becomes fuzzy; our connection is slower, and the flow of life becomes heavier.

When we stay on top of all of the things that require our attention, we keep the vortex clean. Our desires and dreams flow to us with more velocity. When our channel to source energy is filled up with a long list of subconscious things that remain undone, our ability to connect to our dreams becomes foggy. Imagine yourself driving through a snowstorm; you remember where you're going, you see the destination in your mind, but it's just going to take a lot longer to get there!

Keep up with all the things that require your attention so that they don't take up room in your manifestation bubble. Keep it simple by keeping up. Take care of things before they build up! When the slate is clean, you are able to choose what to focus on. When you choose your area of focus, the Universe delivers it!

Even though you might think of yourself as a beginner at manifesting your dreams, expect miracles to happen! Stay in motion as you become clearer on your dreams and allow them to grow beyond those limiting boxes that you live in. You will have to put effort in, as you will notice things being asked of you, things that scare you; do it anyway. When you feel like you can't do it; do it anyway. You will want to give up. Do it anyway! If your dreams don't scare you, they aren't big enough.

You must act when you are called into action. It is the part of the equation that lets the Universe know that you are serious. Everything is given to you at the perfect time, trust that it's on its way and keep up when it comes!

Universe's Insight: "Happiness = Health. If you don't feel healthy, first look at what beliefs you hold that are making you unhappy. Being unhappy will deprive you of your health very quickly."

How Do I Get in the Game?

In this game of life, are you standing on the sidelines watching? Perhaps you're sitting in the stands, or maybe you stayed at home and prefer to watch the game through someone else's experience. Or maybe you are one of the people on the field, jumping into action and going for it.

I can tell you this: the person on the field will surly feel more success because they are in action. They may not score every goal, but they will have a sense of giving it everything they've got. And that is what it will take. When you are following your dreams, things are fun—and they do come easy, but you still have to work at it to make it happen! You have to take action constantly.

Right now, at this very moment, what can you do that will put you on the field? We're talking about your dreams, and if they're big, you'd better get your gear on and go out giving it everything you've got. And don't give up, ever. Be ready to share your gift with the world—the world is waiting for you! Can you believe that? The whole world, seven billion people, and the whole energetic Universe is waiting for you to come into your power.

Get Your Head & Body In The Game

You might hear a coach say get your head in the game to a player on the sidelines or doesn't seem to be focused on the game. A focused player knows where the ball is at all times. He's calling to his teammates, "I'm open, I'm open, give it to me!"

With a focused player there is communication, speed, and receptivity. A focused player is a valuable player. A good team captain knows who to put in the game, who will give it their all.

Be the team captain of your own life: direct it, set it up, create a plan, and follow through. And most importantly, have fun! Enjoy the game; praise yourself for even the smallest accomplishments. A good captain knows how to inspire the team. And a good leader will lead a team to the win. I want you to win. I want us *all* to win! When you win, the whole world wins—the whole Universe wins. And you get to live your biggest dreams!

Get your head in the game and play like a leader.

You will succeed!

As long as you are in the game and focused, there is no way you can lose. You were born to play this game; you know what you have to do, so do it and don't let anything get in the way! Go baby, Go! I want to see you fly!

What's in your Blueprint? Understanding the cycle that keeps repeating itself.

In my blueprint, or my subconscious, I hear the voice that is critical of what I am dreaming. It says, "You, a writer? What a joke! You can't spell, you're a horrible public speaker, you need training, you'll have an anxiety attack." I worried that I would have stage fright (which I don't), as people around spoke a lot about stage freight growing up.

My mother had a number of fears: driving fears (a fear I share), a fear of heights. My sister was afraid of spiders and worms. As a tomboy, I loved catching and playing with worms and spiders. One day, almost as if my sister's fears had become my own, I developed a fear of spiders and worms, too. These were all learned fears; they weren't real.

What I'm getting at here is that we can't even begin to overcome our fears until we see where they have come from. At times, these fears aren't even our own; instead, they have been ingrained into our subconscious memory, and what is available on the other side is not even accessible because we can't see past what stops us.

If you were on a journey and you came upon a brick wall that was one hundred feet high, and as long in each direction as your eye could see, would you stay there determined to find a way over it, or would you turn around and forget about that journey altogether and start to plan a new one?

The problem is that on this new journey guess what comes up? You guessed it: the same wall. This is what our subconscious thoughts do to our dreams. This is why we see so many people with big dreams talking about them, even starting them, but never finishing. These people are stopped at the same point over and over and over again. It's their invisible brick wall. Some call it the glass ceiling.

Here is the difference between somebody who turns their dreams into reality and somebody who doesn't; the dream maker figures out a way to get over the wall—calls in helpers, does whatever it takes to get over the wall—while the other person, the one who continually fails to succeed, doesn't even see that there is another option. Instead, they give up. This is the only difference.

If you can't see the other option, you will always give up. The feeling of success comes from overcoming one of these brick walls, from a confidence of you knowing that nothing will get in the way. The first step is admitting what it is that flows through you freely, effortlessly, and while there is a huge amount of dedication and work involved in making your dreams a reality, it doesn't feel like work because it is your calling; it is what is alive inside you to share. So let me ask you: are you ready *to go big?*

Universe's Insight: "Why don't you believe that you deserve to be happy? You are worthy of joy, abundance, fun, and love, but you make everything so serious that you make yourself feel guilty for the choices you make

that support your own happiness. You have indeed missed the point of being alive. Your purpose for being here is to figure out how to experience the most happiness. Here's a hint: your happiness cannot come from anybody else. Nothing is hard, unless of course you say it is."

Design Your Life!

The life you are living now is a result of the choices that you have made in the past. In the same way, the decisions that you make right now will create the life you'll have tomorrow. So if the choices that you make today affect your life tomorrow, what do you want to create? What are you working on now? A new job, fulfilling a passion, finding a lover, letting go of a lover, becoming an entrepreneur, a stock broker, an accomplished artist, an author, a poet, a singer? What are you thinking about right now? Are you setting yourself up to be happy? Are you setting yourself up to win? Are you acting in a positive way towards making the life you want happen? Can you take full responsibility for the decisions you've made so far?

BUCK UP!

"Buck up" was something that my grandmother used to tell us when we were feeling down, and it always worked for me. Sometimes people need to hear things out loud in order to understand how to break through the fog of their own negative and limiting thought patterns. When we become an observer of our own thoughts, we can see how yin and yang our thoughts can be—we begin to realize our own insanity! Choose what you want to focus on and you will see the object of that focus turn into reality.

From the divine grace of my beautiful grandmother, Tish Girroir: *"Buck up!'*

Expressing Happiness

We are a civilization that is deprived of happiness. The truth is that you deprive yourself, but you have had considerable training and help along the way. The next time you are in a busy area, do some focused people watching. How many of them are laughing? How many are? How many smiles do you see? Count them. Notice what the general consensus is? So why is this such a prevalent deprivation?

Why Are You So Unhappy?

I think that the reason we are deficient in the production of happy brain chemicals is because most of us were never taught how to be happy! We never learned how to master the art of expressing happiness. I still have an extremely hard time fully expressing any emotions, and I'm a pretty emotional person.

Sooner or later we manage to squeeze the joy out of everything. It's time to get your happy on!

Can You Fully Express Your Happiness?

Sometimes I wonder what my reaction would be if I won the lottery—you know, thirty million dollars! Would I jump in the air screaming like a mad woman, or would I quietly call somebody and show tones of excitement without allowing my full joy, excitement, gratitude, freedom, happiness, and craziness to be expressed?

What would you do? Be brutally honest. The first time I thought about how I would react, I felt like I would do the obvious: scream, jump, scream some more, and throw a big party! I don't know what I would do for sure because it hasn't happened yet. We can't really know how we will react to something until it happens. But generally, we react to things the same way over and over again. This is why you get more of what you already have. Your actions and reactions are programmed based on past learning and subconscious programming.

We have been trained not to experience 'big happiness'; in fact, we settle for what we have because we believe this is just the way life is—even when this makes us terribly unhappy.

Happiness and settling are totally different in how they are experienced from an emotional standpoint. And they are both an outcome of the actions you take daily. Happiness fills you, while settling takes away from you. We have been programmed to accept settling, to live our lives in the settling stage. After a while in this stage, you lose your magic; your light dims, and life itself starts to feel like a big struggle. You must take action toward your new dreams in order to change this cycle.

In a way, what we settle for is unhappiness disguised as happiness.

"Trust only movement. Life happens at the level of events, not of words. Trust movement." - Alfred Adler

Universe's Insight: 'Make feeling good a priority. Sometimes what feels good isn't what looks good to others. Allow yourself to be the judge of what feels good to you.

Relearn what happiness is and make yourself so happy that the people around you become happy just by being in your presence."

Make Love to Your Mind

Create within yourself a mind filled with thoughts that feel so good that you can't help but smile. Smile from a deep place, the place of ecstasy!

When you are not feeling healthy, examine what aspects of your life may be taking away from your happiness. Happiness is a state of joy; as such, let happiness be your measure of health. You might live a very long life and have a clean bill of health by medical standards. You might do it all: run 10 kilometers every day, eat lots of fruit and vegetables, avoid drinking coffee, omit gluten and dairy and sugar from your diet. You don't smoke or drink, and you go to yoga daily.

Wow, you really seem to be a model of health. On the outside you look like the healthiest person alive; however, on the inside you feel limited. Your friends have disappeared because you really aren't any fun to be around. Your life is about health instead of happiness. I'll let you in on an insight I had the other day. I was sitting in our brand new car and my soul was exploding with this deep sense of happiness. Suddenly I heard the words *I am healthy because I am happy*. Wow, I thought, now that's a health care regime I can keep up with!

That same day I saw this anonymous quote on Facebook that said, "Create a life that feels good on the inside, not one that just looks good on the outside." It doesn't matter if I live to be 110 or 36; if the moments of my life are filled with happiness and love, each moment is worth its time. The length of my life is not as important as the quality of my life. I live for joyous, pleasurable experiences.

Get On Top of Your Purpose and Ride It

Start living on purpose. By this I mean get on top of your purpose and ride it like a wave, letting it carry you to new destinations. When you see and understand your purpose, make your life complement it. Make changes and adjustments to allow purpose to take over. Let it become you, let it sweep you off your feet and carry you. Get on purpose!

Actions Speak Louder than Words

Actions create results and experiences that words alone cannot." Although words are amazing and have the ability to change the vibration of the entire Universe, observe your actions. I hear people talking all the time about how to make the Earth a better place: how organics are better than GMOs, how people should do something this way and not that way.

The difficulty I see here is that the vibration of what they are saying is not a vibrational match to how they are acting. As Gandhi so cleverly put it, "Be the change you wish to see in the world." *Be* the change! In other words, be the action of what you wish to experience in the world. Don't just talk about change. If you only speak with no action, you might have a bit of success, but when you are in action you create a movement.

Being in action takes more discipline and focus than talking about something. It's easy to talk about removing sugar from your diet; it's another thing to actually do it. It's easy to talk about writing a book—I did it for twenty years!

It's a whole different ballgame to create the time to write the book, find an editor, find an agent, make a book proposal, and get the book published. The experience of talking about writing a book is completely different from the experience and action of writing a book. Talking about something is like watching a football game on TV, while actually writing the book is like being a player on the field.

Being in action is all about being a VIP player in your game of life.

Universe's Insight: "Your actions become your character. Let your words become a by-product of the experiences you have as an outcome of your actions. This way you become a teacher; your words are not just empty words.

When your words are filled with the passion of experience led by action, you become a beacon of knowledge. You are a by-product of your actions. If you want somebody to trust you, you might tell them "you can trust me," but when you prove your trustworthiness to them via your actions, there is a different level of trust reached. If you say you are a hard worker, but your actions show that you are not, it doesn't take long for somebody to notice that what you say and what you do don't match up. Who you are, the way that people experience you, and how you are seen in the world is judged by your character, and your character is built upon your actions.

Do your actions support the person that you know you are? Are you building a character that is a vibrational match to how you want to grow?"

Goal Setting - The Power of Timelines

It is fun to dream about things, and sometimes the dream is all we want to experience before we move on to something else. If you are determined, however, to make something happen, give yourself a timeline, a firm deadline. Maybe you first focus on giving yourself a timeline for the first step, then the next step and the next, until you reach the final date to finish your project.

The brain loves timelines! What seems to happen in life is that other people create timelines for us. Just look at your job; even your schedule is a type of timeline. It's structure. We talk about children needing structure when they are small. As adults, we need structure as well. With structure we focus better, and on a deep level and we love to be focused beings. When we are not focused, we become bored, waste our time, and life loses its meaning.

Your meaning in life comes from your focus, and your focus needs structure to persevere. Some of the best structures are timelines to keep you on track so that you complete tasks and reach your goals. If you look back on your life, you will see that most things that you manifested had some sort of timeline in your mind. Now that you can consciously choose what you want and when you want it, there is only one thing you might have trouble doing: sticking to your timeline—sticking to your word.

When you are in the action of consciously creating your dreams, what you say and do become incredibly powerful forces. Get yourself a to-do list book. Every day before you go to bed, create a to-do list for yourself for the next day. The next day, do your best to complete all the tasks on the list. Do not throw the lists away. You will see very quickly how much you can do. Remember that you are an amazingly incredible being that can accomplish *anything*.

When you are clearing the to-do list daily, you create a clear channel for the Universe to deliver new inspirations. If you don't work with timelines and to-do lists, you risk having a million things floating around taking up headspace and your channel will be blocked.

New inspirations will be unable to come through. You become a mental tornado, and you certainly won't get as much done. You'll forget things and have to do the same things over again many times in order to accomplish this mental list.

This is akin to going to the grocery store for toilet paper, milk, and bread and getting home without the bread and toilet paper, going back to the store and getting sidetracked, getting home and realizing you have bread but no toilet paper. The third time you go to get what you need, you get sidetracked by an old friend you run into in the coffee aisle. You end up going for a coffee to catch up; later, when you get home, you realize that you forgot to get toilet paper again!

Although the coffee with your friend was well worth your time, you have now wasted a great deal of energy and time trying to accomplish one step, falling behind on the other things on your list. This can trigger a storm of negative self-talk; you feel rushed to finish your tasks and sometimes just give up altogether. If you want to be successful at anything, you have to use timelines. The most inspiring and successful people that I know are always in action, always clearing the channel, and always writing new to-do lists.

I like to map out the times that I will do things throughout the day because what I'm actually doing is giving myself little mini timelines. This makes it much easier for me to stay on track. I have learned to love the feeling of checking off my to-do lists. I also love to look back in my to-do list book and see how far I've come, see all the steps that came one after the other that, in the beginning, I couldn't even see. The channel is clear, so more inspiration moves to me and through me.

Stick to Your Word

When you say you are going to do something, do it. When you say you will be there, be there (and be there on time!) Are you aware of how powerful your word is? When you tell somebody that you are going to do something, they count on you to do it. If you don't do it, there is a disconnection on how the flow of the project will go, even if it's as simple as taking out the garbage.

In other words, when you say you will do something and don't do it, you are tampering with the system. Now somebody else has to do it, and the communication is not clear. When you say you will be somewhere and decide not to show up, you completely mess up the energy. Let's say your friend is having a dinner party and you said that you would go, but at the last minute you decide that you would rather stay home and chill out. Well, what you don't know is that the friend throwing the dinner party has a mental vision of who will be there and how it will go, has maybe even invited other people because she is expecting you to be there. Believe it or not, you're a big deal, and when you don't show up the whole party is different.

Your presence makes a difference. Your absence also makes a difference. You create who you are by how well you keep your word. People figure out very quickly whether they can count on you to do what you say you will do, and if you will show up when you say you will show up.

The other powerful part to this equation is to become comfortable saying no to the things that you know you don't want to do. These are the things that you will end up not showing up for anyway. By saying no to the things that you know you don't want to do; you demonstrate a greater integrity to your word. People will come to respect you as somebody who means no when they say no, and they will know that when you say you will be there, you will be. The channel is clear and your relationships with everyone in your life will feel good.

I'm grateful somebody taught me this powerful tool before I had a child. When I speak to Noah, he knows I mean business.

If I tell him he can play a video game for twenty minutes, I will tell him when twenty minutes is up and he puts the game away.

When we are at a park playing and I say we are leaving in five minutes, we leave in five minutes—that's that.

He has never had a tantrum (besides once in the grocery store when he was two) because I am constantly giving him timelines and I always keep my word. He knows me not as a stern mother; instead, he sees me as somebody who means what they say. He counts on me for it, and he's learned the value of it himself.

As a seven-year-old boy, my son created a timeline to make $1,000 over a summer selling lemonade at the local market. At $700 he said, "I kind of want to stop." I told him that he could stop whenever he wanted, but asked him to remember his goal, see how close he was to it, and remember his own words. "The decision is yours," I told him. He promptly said, "I want to keep going! I want to make enough to take you and papa out for dinner and still have $1,000 in my bank account." And our dinner out was beautiful. He paid $75 for it, but the best part as his mother was to experience how proud he was of himself for accomplishing his goal. I was so proud of him for sticking to it so that he could feel this sense of accomplishment.

Whether the goal is money, distance, time, or some other measurement of progress, I notice that people always tend to give up when they are closer to the finish line. Something must happen inside that says, "I guess I'm close enough," and somehow justifies the "I can stop now" voice. More important than how your word affects others is understanding how keeping your word affects *you*. On the flip side, notice how it affects you when you don't keep your word. The first leaves you empowered, and the second leaves you feeling regretful. So what do you want to fuel up on: empowerment or regret?

The Power to Heal through Action

About two years ago I started to get an itchy rash on my fingers and hands; it would drive me crazy! After weeks with no relief and my hands starting to crack open, I went to a doctor who gave me some steroid cream. It worked like magic, and I had no rash or itch for a week. Then it came back itchier and redder than ever, so I fell into a schedule of putting the cream on every few days so that I didn't have to bear that itch.

A year went by, and although the cream eased the itch and cracking and blistering rash, if I didn't put it on for a while the rash would be back in full force.

I asked a lady at a nearby health food store if she could recommend something for the rash. She showed me a topical cream, but also took me over to the book section of the store and told me about her experience with eczema. She advised me to read an entry on eczema in a book she pointed out. When I read it, something resonated with me.

I'm sorry I can't remember the name of the book, but it was about finding the underlying cause of different diseases and illnesses. My interpretation of the page about eczema was that there was something itching to get out of me, and the cracking was a sign that something was trying to bust out of me, not unlike a reptile shedding its skin.

I couldn't think of anything that needed to bust out of me— sometimes we are unaware of what it is. Everything changed when I started writing! After a month of full-on writing, I realized that my eczema had vanished and I hadn't used any cream at all. Once I realized this, it made sense; my fingers had been asking to write, my hands needing to express my soul. Now when I get a small itchy spot I think, I guess it's time to write! And when I do, it goes away.

Our bodies are communicating with us, giving us messages. When something shows up in our bodies that might be uncomfortable, it could be a message leading you to a new understanding. Listening and talking to the body is very powerful! We have so much power within us, there are miracles happening everywhere—you're a miracle maker.

Universe's Insight: "If your actions remain only words, you're coming from a place of the mind. The mind is very powerful, but when your actions come from the heart there is a whole new paradigm of what is possible. Your heart has a huge energy field. Action from the heart will take you on a journey that your mind could never predetermine. The actions that come from the heart are the essence of your soul being expressed in this world.

One way to make sure your manifestations are of the heart is to take what you want and ask, how can this help people? What do you have to give that will make a difference for others and the world? Now, that's a world worth living in. How do your actions feed the mass consciousness? How are your actions feeding you? Are you enjoying the person you have become? Are you experiencing love? Let your life be one of service, and let your service be rooted from your heart. When your heart is leading your life, the Universe opens up to you because it feels your genuine purpose to serve. Whatever it is that you want to achieve, first ask yourself, how can I be of service to others? And then go and do that."

The Action of Love

Most relationships are based on the words 'I love you,' but if we have never been taught how to feel love, how can we really give it? Even more importantly, how can we receive it? Love has become meaningless because we think that just because we say I love you, the other person feels this love. Love that is given with intention and received with your whole being is a whole different kind of love.

If you want to show somebody that you love them, use actions. The words I love you are almost meaningless if the actions of love don't exist. Wouldn't it be interesting if when somebody said they loved us, instead of saying these empty words back we said, "Show me." I know I love being in love; I love the actions of love, I love giving love, I love receiving love. I love experiencing love. I love the action of love. The words are sweet, but the action of love is extraordinary. And why wait for love to magically appear from some outside source? Make an effort to create time for self-love. Make love to your life!

Embrace the feeling or thought that you have won the lottery. Imagine that you hit the jackpot the day you were born, simply because you get to be you; you get to share your song with the world! This is your time. Serve and inspire others by stepping into the energy vibration that you are. Because you my friend, are worth celebrating.

"There is a vitality, a life force, an energy, a quickening that is translated through you into action, and because there is only one of you in all time, this expression is unique. And if you block it, it will never exist through any other medium and will be lost." ~ Martha Graham

Bar-Headed Geese - A Poem by Cindy Gibson Leblanc

Bar-headed geese fly

over the Himalayas, even Everest,

to gain the jet stream:

110 mile per hour tail winds – Godspeed.

Lifted, strung along, prayer flags shredding below,

bar-headed geese endure altitude hypoxia beyond human capacity.

Wing blades resist icing by fierce internal fire,

large wings, fashioned by patient evolution to fly effectively in thin air.

No soaring, or gliding, or useful updrafts carry them aloft:

bar-headed geese flap relentlessly.

Powered along by aerodynamic avian musculature,

undeterred by shearing crosswinds, guided by acute inner navigation,

bar-headed geese instinctively gauge drift to remain on course.

Over the snowy roof of the world in only 8 hours with little to no rest,

a two-month migration from India to Mongolia,

bar-headed geese arrive honking, have made it to the other side.

Some say bar-headed goose ancestors,

alive during the dinosaur dynasty,

flew these routes before Earth buckled

mountain obstacles into their path.

Stately Demoiselles cranes,

Sleek, elegant arrows, red-eyed fliers,

Travel comfortably to the same destination

by mountain passes.

Fascinated, humbled by their unswerving devotion,
determination and stamina,

I credit bar-headed geese with human virtue

While many would claim mere adaptability,

Cite a lack of intelligence in not seeking an easier way: fly
with the cranes?

Humans are so clever, intelligent,

Yet how often do we persevere in the face of adversity

Instead of veering off course to some easy way out,

Throwing away the chance to grow stronger in our own
good faith?

Bowing to nature, steady and wise in her course,

I take inspiration where it shows up,

grateful that she points out exactly who to follow,

as the thrust of ancient geology,

arcs my foundation skyward,

I follow the singular plume of intent to altitude,

would be honored to count myself

in the ranks of bar-headed geese.

-Cindy Gibson Leblanc

My friend Cindy Gibson is a very talented Poet and writer. Thank you for these wise words on strength and action!

"Remember that you are a strong and powerful being— so act like a strong and powerful being."

CHAPTER 9 BECOME HUNGRY AND OBSESSED

HOW BAD DO YOU WANT IT?

"Whatever we plant in our subconscious mind and nourish with repetition and emotion will one day become reality"
~ Earl Nightingale

Universe's Insight: "Obsession is a form of meditation; when we repeat what we want over and over again, the universe listens and delivers with greater speed. Repetition of thought is a law that people have been using since the beginning of time. When we are learning something new or studying something, we repeat it over and over until it becomes something we know. It becomes a habit, and we become what we think! The more we think a thought, the faster it comes. So my advice is to get obsessed about what you love and call it into you. And trust that it's on its way!"

Have you ever wanted something so badly you could feel it in your body? Have you ever been hungry for something? Well, chances are good that if you wanted it that much, you probably got it. Often we have been told along the way to let it go, it'll never happen, and so we give up.

Take a moment to think about somebody that you look up to, somebody that inspires you, somebody that has accomplished many successes. I think of Albert Einstein, Gandhi, some of the great Yogis, Madonna, Donald Trump, and my son Noah. All of these people, although very different minds, have one thing in common: they became hungry for something and allowed their minds to become obsessed with it.

Do you think that Albert Einstein just sat back and let the equation $E = MC^2$ magically appear? No, he worked practically on the same equation for more than ten years with many challenges, many opportunities to give up, yet he never gave up. Eventually he got what he was looking for. Likewise, Gandhi was totally obsessed; he never gave up. The thought of giving up didn't exist in his mind! He became his obsession and he changed the world forever.

You must allow your hunger to become your obsession and allow your obsession to become your character. You become your thoughts and actions. So answer this question: who do you think you are? To figure out what it is that makes you jump for joy from the inside out, we first have to answer a few questions about ourselves. What did you want to be when you were a child? It doesn't matter if you feel connected to this dream at all now; these questions work in an almost magical way, and all you have to do is answer them honestly with raw truth.

Question one: when you were a child, what did you want to be? When you were young, how did you spend most of your time—TV, drawing, playing, singing, competing, sleeping, with family, alone, with friends? You'll notice as you think about this that you're still that person on the inside. Through these simple questions, you are beginning to tune in to who you are instead of who you've learned to be. What activities give you the most energy? What activities seem to drag you down? When are you the most content? What brings you a deep sense of happiness?

When you were growing up, who had the most influence on your decision- making? Did you feel pressured to do things, to fit in, to be more popular? Who did you admire growing up, and why? As a teenager, did you feel supported by your family or ignored? Did you play a lot? What things were important to you when choosing friends? Did you love yourself? Did you learn tools that empowered you? Were you taught to be proud of yourself? We're you told that you could have anything you wanted? Did you do we'll in school? Did you believe that you were smart? Do you believe it now? Did your family struggle with money?

Write down anything else that comes up for you. This is a huge chance for you to begin to see where limitations began creeping into your mind, and where you started to believe your thoughts until they became your reality. This is the structure of your present blueprint. This reality is the life you live now. So, how do you get from here to there—from the life you live now to believing and achieving your largest dreams? The answer is quite simple; are you willing to commit to fifteen minutes a day? If it means completely changing your life and achieving the most unreachable goals and being superstar successful in your life, would you commit fifteen minutes a day to retraining your mind?

What you rethink, you become. It is to your great benefit to choose the thoughts that you want to have playing continuously in your subconscious. In case you haven't noticed, there are thoughts that play over and over again like a movie or even a broken record. In fact, you have probably had the same thoughts playing for many, many years. Are you even aware of them? I recommend taking some time to get to know what these constant subconscious thoughts are.

First, spend fifteen minutes a day listening. Don't try to break up the chatter of your mind or stop it. Listen honestly, openly, and unattached, as if you were sitting and listening to a good friend talking. When your friends are talking to you openly and honestly, they are not always looking for advice; often they just want to be heard. Being heard is all these thoughts want.

They have been running over and over and over again for who knows how long and you've unconsciously avoided listening to them.

You may think this doesn't apply to you, but the truth is that you avoid listening to these deep subconscious thoughts because they can be painful, not nice at all—like your own internal bully. These thoughts can be very negative: you're stupid, ugly, nobody likes you. They're all way better than you, you'll never do that, you don't deserve it, you're not good enough.

I recommend taking out your journal and writing down the honest thoughts that come from the depths that have created your reality so far and will keep running the show until you listen. First you listen, then you re-choose. It works like this from this point on. Listen, re-choose. Listen, re-choose. Listen, re-choose. This is how you retrain your brain and change your life.

When you become obsessed, your mind is focused on a single thing. The conscious and subconscious minds are always scheming, planning ways to create and make things happen. Imagine the mind and your thoughts as a connection to the Universe. All the things you think about are coming to you. The Universe has no choice but to give you what you think about.

For me, it has been writing a book. I've become obsessed with it; I love allowing the passion in my mind body and soul to pour out of my fingers and through my keyboard, manifesting into the very words that you're reading right now. I love the pure source energy that so beautifully flows through me to you. I became obsessed with publishing a book—and trust me, there were a whole armload of reasons that I couldn't be a writer, but I was willing to let those limiting thoughts go. You know the thoughts I'm talking about: the one that says, you, a writer? What a joke! You can't even write a complete sentence. You can't spell. You don't even know what a semicolon is.

And fair enough, these thoughts were true; I didn't love editing, spelling, or making it right. I just loved writing.

As long as I can remember, even as a young party-crazed teenager, all I wanted to do was write a book. I knew what kind of book I would write even at that age. I didn't enjoy fictional novels, and much preferred reading inspiring non-fiction stories. I questioned things as a young teenager—like why do guys and girls behave so differently?

I remember wanting to write my first book about the differences between men and women. About a year later, I found the book Women are from Venus and Men are from Mars. I thought to myself, this is my book!

And then I recall the feeling of how the Universe works quickly, with speed. I felt like I had missed the boat. Someone had already written my book, and I stopped writing for many years. Despite this, I never stopped thinking about being a writer.

I've always told friends over the past twenty years that I would write a book someday, and for them to keep their eyes out for it. It's a kind of knowing; when you know, you know. It's almost like the book is as obsessed with me as I am with it! It's the most glorious feeling I have ever felt: to be called towards something and find myself absolutely obsessed with my purpose!

When you feel called to something you dream about it. These visualizations become vivid and can feel absolutely real. You begin to believe that it's yours, and when you believe it, you see it. It becomes what you think about, what you research, what you discuss with people who inspire you.

After a time, you'll notice that suddenly there are workshops happening, seminars, things beyond your dreams offering themselves freely to you. When you let yourself obsess, you spend your time calling this to you!

Truthfully, if we spent any time listening to our thoughts, we would quickly realize that we are obsessed with something, anyway. You may as well choose your obsession. You already know what you want; start talking to it, invite it to live loudly in your life, let it become who you are!

Universe's Insight: "The things that you are obsessed about, the things that visit in the form of thoughts and dreams over and over again, are not something over which you have control. Consider that these things have chosen you as their vehicle of expression. These repetitive thoughts and dreams are obsessed with you. They have been calling you to be the vehicle, to be the catalyst. These thoughts that call to you are your golden ticket."

Consider that what you have been searching for or dreaming about is also seeking you. Think of your obsession not as a negative thing over which you have no control, but a part of you longing to be expressed. When you immerse your entire being into something, let it be something that you choose and not something that has been chosen for you.

In the world we live in today, there are many things into which we are subconsciously immersed: religions, careers, beliefs about who we should be, how we should act and even how we should look. We are a culture that is obsessed with, being skinny—we can't help but be hooked into a belief that skinny is better, and we've created a whole world of beliefs that justify this for us.

I prefer not to obsess about a skinny, healthy world, and instead look for things that bring me joy. For me, nothing about being skinny makes me happy; in fact, it quickly robs me of my happiness because the underlying self-talk is "what I am now is somehow not good enough." Instead, I became obsessed with letting go of beliefs that don't have a positive impact on my life.

For many years I have been obsessed with changing the way that I think. It is a conscious obsession and it has taken many years of reprogramming my mind, one thought at a time. I gave myself time through conscious awareness and listening meditations focused on understanding my internal dialog. Through this, I quickly became aware of why I felt so sad and hateful. My inner chatter was my biggest enemy. My vibration was very low, making the world a dark place. Even so, I noticed that I had this little light, the voice of a small child saying, I want to experience happiness. I'm sick of feeling this way. I want love, I want Joy, and I want to live a life different than this.

I heard a voice and I made a promise that I would do my best to create these things that I so longed for. It took time and patience and effort, but after months of acknowledging the negative self-talk, I became obsessed with catching these thoughts and replacing them with friendlier, more positive ones. At first this replacement of self-talk felt fake and weird, but I could immediately feel the results of this exercise. So to this day I still am obsessed with uncovering these negative thoughts and replacing them with more helpful ones. It works. I have a completely different life than I did then, and all that changed was the way that I spoke to myself.

Subsequently, everything in my life changed. I got it; I am the creator of my life. I want to choose how it goes and how I feel and what I do. Now, joy is seeking me. What I have come to realize is that all that you desire is within you. You have been taught that you must search outside of yourself to find what you seek. If it wasn't within you, you wouldn't be seeking it in the first place. So why wouldn't you choose to become obsessed about something that you want to obsess about; in this, you become the fruit of this obsession.

Universe's Insight: "Becoming obsessed about something is easier now than it has ever been. You have a world of information at your fingertips. Anything that you want

to become is available. We are living in a world of virtually free technology. Choose it, search it, think it, believe it, create it, and become it. Don't let anything get in the way."

What Connects You to Spirit?

Consciousness, spiritual connection, higher power...what does it all mean? Philosophers identify consciousness as an aspect of the relationship between the mind and the world around us. To writers on spiritual or religious topics, consciousness frequently connotes the relationship between the mind and God, or the relationship between the mind and deeper truths that are thought to be more fundamental than the physical world.

I can only explain this on a level that I have experienced. Consciousness is the energy of the universe, a vibration. Physics says that all things are vibrating with energy. This is how I have experienced consciousness. It is not something that we have or that comes to us suddenly; rather, it is the constant creative energy that flows through everything.

To begin to understand this, you need to understand the difference between finite and infinite. Finite in this context means separate, singular, apart from. When you are disconnected from spirit, you are only you. You see life as yourself against the world, and this represents a low vibration of consciousness. When you are connected to spirit, you feel like you belong; there is a sense of community, oneness, and unity, a connection to something that is flowing through you. You become a channel of the Universal flow of energy. This is a much higher state of consciousness. The vibration in which your mind sees and connects to the world and the Universe is what determines your state of consciousness.

So when looking for what it is that connects you to spirit, ask yourself what makes you feel whole and complete? What allows you to be you, what brings you closer to what's true for you and causes you to stop searching outside of yourself for something? When your conscious vibration is high, you understand that everything is within you and nothing is outside of you.

When you're in the high vibration of consciousness, there is nothing that is impossible because you're able to see the world with infinite eyes. Some people say that I'm a dreamer. Truth be told, I am a dreamer, but I dream from a place of belief that everything that I can possibly grasp in my mind, anything I can visualize, anything I can think of, is ultimately possible. Because the thought and vision that I am having is part of the unfolding of evolution, and I'm simply playing my part.

Who Is On Your Team?

Surround yourself with people who support you. If you want to create wealth, be around wealthy people. If you want to be an artist, connect with people and groups who are creating art. If you love animals, spend time with animals. You get the point. The most important factor in creating your dreams is to surround yourself with people who support and understand your passion. Create a team of people that help you reach your goals, hold you to your word, and offer guidance on the subject. If you want to be a professional basketball player but spend all your time at a bar drinking beer instead of on the court practicing your skills, you will likely become a guy who sits at the bar talking about the game.

Making this a priority in your life might mean letting go of friendships and people who do not add to your dream, and adding to your life people who do. It all depends on how much you want it. If you really want it, the right people will appear to support you. You must trust that the Universe is rooting for you. It supports you and it wants you to win. It will always give you what you need. Build a strong team, and the momentum of your dreams will unfold effortlessly.

Practice using the right muscles in order to strengthen your vision. I was having a discussion with my husband about hard work and how we both thought of hard work in a different way. He started talking about professional athletes and how hard they work—how they work out for thirteen hours a day to be the best they can be. Yes, I acknowledged, but if you were a basketball player who spent eight hours a day working at a bank, you would be exercising the wrong muscles. The same would be true if you dreamed of being a financial adviser but you spent thirteen hours a day working out and playing basketball.

The key is to make your dream a focal point and practice and spend most of your waking time dedicated to learning about and strengthening that muscle. You will find that the work that you put in doesn't really feel like work—well, maybe on those off days, days when you need a push, when the basketball player doesn't want to work out. That's when it feels like hard work. Otherwise, the work just seems to perform itself once you decide and become obsessed; once you become dedicated, the work does itself.

Are you using your time to strengthen the muscle that builds success around your dream reality, or are you filling up your time with things that keep you from reaching your full potential?

When you practice something over and over again, your brain creates new patterns. Let's say that you decide to be an artist, yet you haven't drawn a picture since you were ten. Maybe the thought of painting on a canvas creates anxiety. You could easily be stopped by these thoughts, and probably have been for many years. On the other hand, you could start looking at art, buying different brushes, clay, pencils, paint, and read books about art, talk about art with others interested in the subject.

Soon your hand holds a paintbrush that softly glides across a canvas, and you feel your 'art' muscle getting stronger each time you sit down to paint. You see art with new eyes, and begin to find yourself conversing with other painters. Your whole lifestyle begins to change because you have aligned yourself with your dream of being a painter. I'm not implying that you should quit your job—unless it completely takes away from your dream. So many people get stuck doing a job that has nothing to do with their dream, something they can become very busy at for years and years, something that quiets the thoughts and voices that have been calling to them.

Somehow, deep inside, we believe that if we don't try, we can't fail. And so we go to work, come home, make dinner, clean up, and go to bed. We become so busy living that we no longer hear the call. And so the thoughts and voices of your dharma fade, but they never disappear.

Don't give up! It's always been inside of you; it never leaves. It is there waiting for you to take the first step. You don't need to see the whole staircase. You just need to take the first step.

Make your dream a priority!

It may be hard to believe, but on some level, you are doing exactly what you love. Imagine if the judgments of good or bad, healthy or unhealthy were non-existent.

Now look at your life and see how this is true for you. Stay away from content about the future; sure, what you're doing now brings you joy, but it is never going to help you become a successful actor. There is only right now, this very moment. The soul will always move towards what brings you joy in this moment.

If somebody is giving you flak about something (which doesn't feel good), you may find yourself sourcing out friends to have fun with or finding something else that brings you a more joyful feeling. I've come to believe that this is what's really going on in the background of addictions. I don't really like the word addiction because it's a word that was created to put us in a box when we consistently indulge in something that on some level contributes to bring us joy.

We have a disease, they say (whoever *they* are), but when this thing that we are addicted to stops bringing us joy, trust that your body mind and soul will walk away and find a different source of joy.

This leads me to believe that the reason we have so many people suffering from addiction is because we don't allow ourselves joy. Most things that bring us joy are taken away from us as children—from food to friends. Somehow we have managed as a species on this planet to take everything that tastes delicious, feels good, and brings laughter and joy and lifts our spirits and have made it wrong. We squeeze the joy out of all these things. What we are left with is a feeling of emptiness, a longing, and we turn to anything that will bring us instant feelings of joy, belonging, love, and most of all, acceptance. This habitual place where we find joy often becomes an "addiction."

So, why don't we learn how to bring joy into our lives? Why is this not part of our curriculum? It would be beneficial to learn joy-enhancing techniques in school so that we feel joy inside despite any outside situations. We are full and complete without the need to look outside for these feelings to be fulfilled. Believe that your true nature has always guided you in the direction of what felt good in any given moment.

Now you have the knowledge of choice.

"Make It Your Life, Get Obsessed With Your Passion"

CHAPTER 10 SUCCESS

POUR THE CHAMPAGNE BABY

When you have an attitude of success, the rest of the world sees you as successful. When you have a losing attitude, the rest of the world sees you as a loser. Even if you have tried and failed but have an attitude of success, the world will see you as successful. What you think, you become.

The important principle to remember is that you will have moments of failure on the road to success; these are what make the journey worthwhile; this is what makes it so exciting when you win. If you always won, it wouldn't feel like winning. It would become average. Although it sounds like a great way to live, I promise that you would get bored very quickly!

Humans love to be challenged. Chances are that if you knew you would win every time, you would stop trying. Enjoy the contrast of winning and losing, but never give up! I use this saying with my son: if plan A doesn't work, there are still 25 other letters in the alphabet!

Define Your Success

What would success look like to you? What would it feel like? Feel successful now. Change the way you think about it! When you say I want to be successful, it becomes something you are reaching for, like enlightenment—which is fine, but you aren't going to find it "out there somewhere." Enlightenment and success are found *inside.*

People who have a successful personality get hired faster, are more confident, and aren't bogged down with worry.

They are optimistic and happy. Success really is all about confidence. And confidence isn't something you can buy; it's something you know. Some people have had the advantage of being brought up by parents that had positive, confidence building, be anything, do anything attitudes. Others have been raised in a way that didn't support their dreams; they were told 'no' a lot. Their parents struggled to make ends meet, and the attitude was generally about survival.

The former group might have an easier time with this philosophy because thinking big and knowing that their dreams are reachable has been naturally ingrained; you might even say that they were raised to be successful. The latter group might find this philosophy unrealistic and unattainable. Both groups, though, have the power to choose, and both will have the experience of winning and losing as they move through life.

Success doesn't have to be about money or reaching a particular end result. Success is about loving what you're doing in every moment. If you're waiting to be successful, you will find that you will always be stuck, waiting to be successful. Even after the house, the cars, the vacation homes, the perfect job, the assistant, and the personal chef, there will always be something more to reach for.

On the other hand, if your success comes from within, you won't have to keep reaching. You might keep receiving, but you won't have to strive for the success. This kind of success will never disappear or be taken away because it comes from you, from being you, alive, here, now! And that is true success.

I love this quote by Abraham from Ester Hicks, "The standard of success in life isn't the things. It isn't the money or the stuff - it is absolutely the amount of joy you feel."

Graciously shared from The Daily Law of Attraction Quotes

Abraham-Hicks, © by Esther Hicks,

AbrahamHicks.com

(830) 755-2299.

Put your "SOMEDAY'S into action!

We've all heard the saying "someday never comes," and to be quite frank, it doesn't! If you are dreaming about what you will have someday, you will keep getting further away from what you want because the Universe hears your wish as someday, meaning you are not ready for it now (now being the present moment). And maybe you're actually not ready at all! If that's the case, acknowledge that you're not ready and go back to doing what makes you happy now.

When you feel that you have accomplished something and are excited about it, start to share it with the world immediately—not someday when you're better, someday when it's perfect, someday when you have more training, more practice, more money, more time. Guess what? Someday never comes because "someday" becomes the habitual context in which you keep your dream at bay.

The first thing that you should realize is that when you use the thought or word "someday," it's actually a roadblock, It's an excuse that you use to not allow the flow *now*. What you're really saying to the Universe is *not now, maybe later*. And this *someday* language gradually becomes your future. You actually live a "Someday Life," which becomes a life filled with regret.

If I can offer one piece of advice to you, it would be this: let go of your addiction to "someday" and take the next step (even if it's small) and do what you can do now. Put "someday… into *action*." All of the things you feel you need to do become roadblocks at first; the more there are, the stronger the block. I still deal with these things all the time, but instead of letting them block my path, I see them as a gift because I know that on the other side of the block is a huge breakthrough. So instead of giving up and letting my project die inside of me, I ask "what *can* I do right now?"

There always is a next step, even though you often see these same roadblocks over and over again. Most of the time we are unconscious of them and we tend to give up. We begin another attempt at accomplishing a goal, and then another unconscious roadblock comes along and we give up yet again.

In order to experience something you've never experienced before, you're going to have to *do* something you've never done before. So how do you work up the courage to share yourself? How can you become vulnerable?

Well, first you need to start. If you sing, sing for somebody; put yourself out there. If you're an artist, have an art show. One way to gain the inward feeling of success is to gain confidence, and when you share what you do, people will start to feed that success. Post it on Facebook or YouTube. Talk to people about it. Build up your success support.

When you are living with passion, people are attracted to the energy that you carry. They want to receive what you are sharing. People who are living and sharing their passion with the world—no matter how popular they become— always have a strong feeling of success. Benjamin Disraeli who was born over 200 years ago put it this way: "One secret of success in life is for a man to be ready for his opportunity when it comes". So one might want to change their habitual language from "someday" to *I'm ready for the next step!*

Walk Your Talk

Dress the dress, talk the talk; begin to exude an aura of success in your field. Watch and listen to the people who inspire you and notice how they carry themselves. Have a vision of what you look like in your mind's eye as successful in what you want to do or be. Practice the Alpha meditation we described in the Create and Jump chapter. Hold a vision of what success looks like on you and really examine it--what are you wearing, how are you speaking, how you feel, how you hold your body, who you surround yourself with, and what sort of meetings you attend.

Now start making that a reality. Go buy some new inspiring clothes, hold yourself confidently, practice speaking to people about what you do, invite people to meetings or pot lucks to discuss things related to your vision of success. This is being in the *now* of success; there is no "someday" in the present. Once you start to reinvent yourself, your success will be pouring out of you. People around you will be astounded at your transformation. You may even catch a glimpse of yourself in the mirror and say, "Wow, who is that?" Successful people have successful thoughts. Train your brain to have successful thoughts.

Are you the kind of person who asks for what you want and need? Or are you the kind of person who walks uncomfortably through life wishing and allowing others to create change because you expect them to simply know that you're uncomfortable and unhappy?

This is not how a successful person lives. As a person who is creating success in life, you have to get used to asking people for what you want and need. News flash: people can't read your mind! Use your voice and tell people what you need. Be clear and concise. If you are serious about making something happen, you're going to have to dig deep into your confident voice and let people know clearly what you need, want and desire.

When you don't tell people what you want and need and desire, you create an energy system called "The Guessing Game." Sometimes they get it right, but most of the time they get it wrong—and then you get angry because they didn't do it right. You blame them. Has this ever happened to you? Next time this situation arises, notice your own neurosis and your lack of clarity. Blame yourself for not being clear. Take responsibility for your life. Try taking the rap by saying, "I'm sorry, I should have been clearer about that. My bad; I'll be clearer next time."

Would you go for a massage and lie down on the massage table and try to massage yourself? Of course not. However, would you sit through an hour-long massage that felt uncomfortable or painful without saying a word? Would you stay in a relationship or marriage that no longer made you happy? Would you stay at a job where you were not appreciated? Would you hold on to friends who spoke negatively about you?

If you said yes to any of these, take a moment and ponder…why? What keeps you from being a strong, vibrant person? The answer is *you!* The only reason you let negative situations go on and on for a long period of time is because you have become a coward in your own life; you're playing a small game. Now that you're aware of that, you can strengthen your power. Start cutting the garbage out of your life and play on a higher level, a level that empowers your soul!

First you have to let go of what you've become accustomed to. Have the confidence to go beyond your comfort level and permit a new perspective of life to move into your awareness. You will see the world with new eyes. Design your life so that it feels good!

When You Are In Alignment with Your Dream, There Is No 'No'!

I was talking to a friend while we were sitting on a bench on a hot sunny May Day after lunch, and she was telling me about how her dream of living by the ocean was starting to unfold beautifully. Jacqueline had been talking about loving the ocean and living by the ocean and for as long as I have known her. Every time we would get together, I wondered if this would be the time that she would tell me that she was moving to the coast. And this was the day!

She said that one morning she woke up and thought, "I'm done." Her present job wasn't panning out, and she decided in that moment that it was time to resign and move to the water. Jacqueline had known for a long time that her dream was to be by the ocean; she was being called to it. For many years she had been trying to delay or avoid that call, but she knew it was there. And as soon as she realized that it was time to listen to the call, she started taking action. She got a new a job, gave her notice at her present workplace, booked flights. Everything seemed to just fall into her lap. Things worked out even better than she had thought possible.

We don't usually see the whole picture in the beginning. She was telling me about how scared she was to tell her family. The need to please and get approval from others comes up so much when we are on this journey, often surfacing when we are trying to get in our own way. Once you *really know,* all of the things that may have stopped you in the past become irrelevant. There is no way you can listen to a 'no.' The mind tries to come up with things to deter you--thoughts like you can't do that, just leave everything, what will your family think, you don't have enough money. The good news is that the volume of these thoughts is not very loud because the force behind the alignment of your dream is so powerful. This force almost seems to guide your fingers to make phone calls, to book tickets, and to do what needs to be done.

When discussing projects and fundraisers, you often hear people say that they seem to "take on a life of their own." In fact, it does. When you say yes to something and the Universe knows that you're 100% in, it takes over. Source is experiencing life through you; it wants to support the path to ultimate happiness, so it starts flooding to you what you need. It feels as though you're just along for the ride, and although the ride might be bumpy, overall it's a very good ride. If the ride you've chosen isn't bringing you a base that feels good, get off this ride, walk down a different path, and discover another of the many rides to choose from. Try something else out from the endless selection the Universe has available just for you!

What is Alignment?

Wikipedia defines body alignment as, "In sports and dance, the proper placement of bones so that muscles do less work." I wanted to share this definition because it shows that when things are in alignment, less work is needed and less energy is expended. When you are in alignment with your dream, everything becomes easier. Things line up and suddenly there is no pushing up against it; instead, you begin to see how everything you have ever done leads to this point, even screw-ups! Start appreciating your mistakes, because they're all part of the plan that is leading you to your destiny. Be grateful for and take to heart the lessons you have learned along the way!

Universe's insight: "When you are in alignment with what brings you joy, there is no suffering."

Start Saying YES!

I try to say yes as much as possible! How often do you say no when something is offered to you? I believe that something offered is a gift from the Universe. Although over the years I haven't been 100% faithful to this theory, I have said yes to many things. Some of these yeses ended up leading to things I couldn't have imagined, and have also, of course, occasionally gotten me into trouble.

One memorable "yes" resulted in a two-day hangover. Sporting a hangover I was not enjoying very much, I thought to myself, "If only there were only a way to filter when you say yes and when you say no!"

In actuality, this filtering does exist; it has to do with listening. When somebody asks you a question or offers you something, instead of a knee-jerk yes or a no, stop and think about it for a moment. Be quick; don't think about it for more than thirty seconds, otherwise you risk overcomplicating it, and the sincerity behind the offer becomes obsolete. If the answer is still yes after a moment in listening, then *go for it!* Even if it were something you would normally say no to, *do it!*

You never know what might happen, who you will meet, or what thoughts and insights this experience will lead to. *Say hello to your new friend and guide, Intuition!*

What would happen if you said *yes* to everything today? Getting out of your own way is the key to letting the flow of success move through you. Let your fears and over-intellectualization take a vacation and just do it. Say yes!

What Is Going to Make You Feel Good Right Now?

There will always be people who don't believe in your dream. It is important to not let their beliefs create an ending for you. The only thing that matters is that you believe in yourself. When you're connected to the highest part of yourself, it doesn't matter what anybody else thinks. A tree doesn't stop being a tree and ask; "I wonder what all the other trees will think of me if I grow three inches today." It reaches proudly for the sun, drinking up as much water as it can so that it can become the strongest and most beautiful tree it can be.

This is what we all want. We all want to become the best that we can be; we shouldn't need permission from anyone else to do so. Reach for what it is that makes you grow, that makes you feel complete. When Madonna was asked why she sang, she answered, "Because if I didn't, I would die." Find that part of you, remember that part of yourself that is life itself, and connect to it. Start walking the walk, talking the talk, and sharing it with the world. It is your ticket to all that you desire. When you are in a place where you are connected to the highest part of yourself, you inspire everything around you to do the same. We are born to be alive, to feel good, and to thrive. Find that knowing inside of yourself and live it.

Nothing Is More Important Than a Moment of Bliss

Rest when it's time to rest, dream when it's time to dream, act when it's time to act, eat when it's time to eat, and sleep when it's time to sleep. When we push things to happen, there is an effort, a pushing against, which creates resistance—an awkward mixture of what you think you should be doing with what you need in this moment.

You could be resisting something that is being offered to you effortlessly. If you jumped into a rubber dinghy and started floating downstream with a strong current and tried to paddle against the current, it would be very difficult; you would most likely give up. When we are not in alignment, this is what we experience: the 'working extremely hard and getting nowhere' syndrome. Everything becomes a chore; life seems to become a struggle.

When we are in alignment, we are floating along, propelled by the current, with the source flowing into and through us. You'll know when this is happening because when this source is flowing through you, you feel good. It's that simple; when you are not aligned with what makes you feel good, you become miserable, rushed, unhappy, and frustrated. You are in alignment when you feel success growing in your life because there is this feeling of being on the right path, a path where things line up for you perfectly and effortlessly.

Universe's Insight: "Do what feels good right now, and if that stops bringing you joy, stop doing it and move in the direction that nurtures you in a more joyful way!"

The power is inside you. When you are unbound by the expectations of others, the power you have is magical and abundant. Unfortunately, we have given our power away in so many ways. The need to be different than we are, the careers we spend unhappy years at crawling to the top of nowhere—why do we do that?

Your power ignites when you are happy and in love with what you do. Your power to create something new starts with a thought; the law of attraction is always working and listening to what it will bring to you. Unfortunately, most of us have been living in an unconscious awareness of what we are creating and focused on what we don't want instead of what we do want.

The Universe brings us what we focus on; the mind is the greatest tool given to us to connect to this omnipresent and endless power of the Universe. Have you ever thought about somebody, and suddenly the phone rings and it's them? This isn't a coincidence; this is the power you have! You can call things into being. If you want peace and solitude and you're thinking about all the reasons why you don't have peace and solitude, you will get more of the stuff that doesn't give you peace and solitude.

I love asking people what their passion is, what they really love, and it surprises me how often people don't know. How have we come to a place in life that we are so absent from our own source of happiness, just going through the motions of living, that we don't know what makes us feel good? I was talking to a girl today and I asked her this question, and she said, "I'm still waiting for that lightning bolt. My doctor says I'll never find it." I didn't ask, but I'm assuming that this lady who seems happy on the outside is filled with sadness and depression. I felt a fury deep in my stomach, but instead of jumping on the negative argument about doctors and prescriptions, I gently responded with the words, "Don't worry, you'll find it."

I know that it's not about *finding* something; rather, it's about *listening* and *following*. Don't ever let anybody tell you that you can't live your dream! People who say such things are usually unhappy themselves and can't see beyond the box that they have been put into. Your power is so strong that it makes the stars glitter in the sky, makes the sun light up the world every day, and makes the human body so perfect with all of its systems working so magnificently in unison. You are worthy of your power, and when you find it, feel it and follow it and you will be free.

Become aware of your power to choose. There are so many people telling us what to believe that we forget that we have a choice. Sometimes it feels as if there is no choice at all; we are told that what we have is reality. Sometimes we are called crazy when we speak about what it is that we choose to believe.

Religion is a perfect example, even though there is nothing to prove but individual experience. We all have our own belief system; some people believe in one God, some believe in many gods, and some believe that there are no gods. Most religions don't give adherents the choice of what to believe; it's their way or no way at all.

Immersed in all the pressure to become a believer of a certain following, we often forget that we do in fact have a choice. I remember being a child of around ten with a Catholic upbringing, and it was time for my Confirmation, a time when you pronounce yourself a believer of God in the Christian faith. I told my mother that I didn't want to do a confirmation. She asked why, and I said I was unsure of my belief, so how could I go forward with the ceremony. Although I'm sure she was taken aback, she agreed and we never spoke about it again. I feel blessed that she gave me the freedom to choose, and this moment in time helped me to become a confident chooser throughout my life.

As a mother myself now, I try to give my son the power to choose. It can be difficult as a parent because you want to control things so that life is manageable and everybody is safe. Giving Noah the freedom to choose has led me to living with an extremely confident seven-year-old boy, and to a miniature zoo in our condo. We have a dog, a cat, a hedgehog, two fish, and are in the process of adding a lizard to the menagerie, all the result of my choice to say yes as much as possible. Our son is also a responsible young boy who has a huge heart and a great respect for life. He has a great sense of success because we have taught him to accomplish his dreams. He doesn't look outside of himself to feel good. He creates a life that supports his own joy!

Take responsibility for the amount of joy you have.

If you feel stuck in life, or a job, with a sickness, in an unfulfilling relationship, or with anything else that makes you unhappy, look back and take responsibility for the choices that you made leading up to this state of affairs. There is no doubt that you have chosen to be where you are. The good news is, you can re-choose anytime you like. This is the greatest gift, the gift to choose—and choose, and choose again.

Always remember that nobody has control over your life, not your boss, your parents, your friends, your spouse… only you can choose your life in every moment. The more conscious you are in your choosing, the more things will work out for you. When you feel stuck, this is a sign that you are not consciously choosing your life. And when you are not consciously choosing what you want, you give your power away. As long as you are giving your power away, you will never experience a real sense of success.

One thing that becomes very important in the conversation about choice is realizing that you also have the ability to choose what you think about and what you focus on. If you spend your time thinking about how poor you are, how you'll never have what others have, and you watch the news that tells you the economy is bad and getting worse, then it is almost certain that you are living a life of scarcity and fear.

If you choose to believe in abundance and generosity and spend your time being inspired by those who are successful and generous, and you are grateful for what you have now, you probably have abundance and love in your life.

You do have a choice to change the channel; you can even turn it off. Choose to be grateful, focus on scarcity or abundance, love or hatred, health or sickness, misery or joy. Just know that what you focus on is what you will see. You can choose to believe anything you want. Think about what kind of person you want to be and what kind of life you want to live. Next, check to see if what you think about, listen to, and do is aligned with what you want; if it's not, start by changing these actions and thoughts so that they better feed your desire. When you are living in a way that feeds your deepest desires, you will feel joy and abundance—and this is the true feeling of success.

Share your success with others. Share your joy with others. Share your wealth, share your love, share your gifts, share your dreams, share your life. You'll see that the more generous you are, the more you will receive.

"Start Celebrating Something Everyday!"

CHAPTER 11 GRATITUDE

GRATITUDE BRINGS YOU MORE THINGS TO BE GRATEFUL FOR

Universe's Insight: "When you can sit in gratitude in a world that seems to squeeze the joy out of everything, you win. When you can find something to be grateful for in the midst of frustration, anger, and pain, you win. When you lie in bed at night and feel grateful for your bed, your pillow, your family, and your life, you win. When you are grateful for the food you eat and enjoy the experience of what food tastes like, you win. When you are grateful for what you wake up to everyday, love what you see, and feel joy in both little things and big things, you win. When you can be grateful for even the worst memories because of the lessons learned, you win. When you become grateful for the world you live in, you win.

At the point of your last breath on this planet, if you are grateful for the life that you have had, you win. Gratitude is your key to happiness. When you look for things for which to be grateful, you become bigger. You connect to the Universe, and the Universe provides you with more to be grateful for. This is a law. If you want to be happy, start with being grateful for what you have now. Focus on what feels good and refuse to focus on the negative. Become immune to negativity. Be strong enough to walk away from negative people or negative situations, and do so because you know it's not worth your time or energy. Realize your worth by being grateful for all that you already have.

A life has been given to you; that alone is something to be grateful for. The fact that you get to experience all of this life in whichever way you choose is something to be grateful for. Be grateful for the contrasts in life. Be grateful for the darkness that allows you to enjoy the light. Smile, knowing that you are untouchable unless you choose to be. Go, be the best you can be, the happiest you can be.

Be crazy, be generous, be strong, know your power— don't *ever* give up on your dreams. Express yourself freely, share your success with the world, be bold, be the catalyst that creates change, have fun, but above all, be you. Believe that you are here for a reason, that you to have a purpose; be grateful for the beauty that is you and know that never again will anybody ever exist with exactly the same set of gifts that you have. Be grateful for the gifts you have been born with. Be grateful that you have this opportunity. Enjoy your time on this planet.

Life is a party; be grateful for all the surprises that have come and all the surprises that are on the way. Be grateful for those that put up with you and don't ask for you to change because they love you the way you are. It is good to be loved. Be grateful for love.

When somebody does something for you from the goodness of their heart, say thank you and really mean it. Feel the expression of gratitude in every cell of your body. Dance because it feels good and be grateful for the freedom. Be grateful for your voice and don't be afraid to use it. Be grateful for the air and breathe it in deep. Be grateful for the insects that pollinate your food and create balance in our world. There is so much to be grateful for.

Be grateful even for the feeling of being grateful. Know that this world will never exist the same way again without you; you are part of the Oneness that is alive right now. You affect all that is with your presence. The stars have a reason to shine every night because you are here to see them. The sun rises for you. The trees make oxygen for you. This life was built for you. Now, *that* is something worthy of gratitude.

Notice every day how the world is grateful for you, because without you, it would have no reason to exist. Thank you, Thank you for being you. You are unique, a physical expression of the Universe which you create— and what a beautiful Universe it is! Take some time every day, every moment, to find the magic, the miracles in life. Make time to experience the feeling of gratitude. Know that you are deeply loved and taken care of."

- The Universe

Acceptance

With all the boxes that we have put ourselves in, it can be hard to remember who we really are. In order to get yourself to a place of knowing what you know you really are, you have to go through a process of elimination. To get back to the pure consciousness that you are, you first have to acknowledge what you are *not*.

You are not your body; your body is your home, your human vehicle, but it is not who you are. This might be a hard one for some of you to grasp because you-as-your-body is all you've learned, and if you are not your body, then what are your legs, your abs, or your hair?

You are likewise not your identities. You are not a mother, father, daughter, son, yogi, businessman, musician, writer, artist, husband, or wife. These are all roles that you play, but they are not who you are.

You are not what you have. We grow up aiming for big things, often informed by what surrounds us growing up. A nice, big house to me might look completely different in my mind than a nice big house might look like to somebody that grew up in the Hamptons. We grow up believing that our value is based on what we have; if we have a mansion and five vacation homes with five cars, we believe that we will be complete and happy.

Unfortunately, our happiness from these outside things only lasts for short periods of time. If people only know you because of what you have, you have completely ripped them off – or they are totally shallow. Your needs become bigger, and you find yourself in a cycle of external happiness and unhappiness. Find your happiness from inside, because if you are getting it from the outside, it can be taken away. If you are not what you have, then who are you?

Endings and Beginnings

As we come to the end of this journey together, I would like to spend a moment in gratitude with you, the reader. Thank you for picking up this book. Thank you for sharing this journey. Now we have this connection that somehow links us together; although we may have never met, we have a mutual understanding of the power that resides within us—the power to accomplish the most impossible things.

We have a strong inner knowing of who we are and what we want, and we will permit nothing to bring us down or get in the way of our success and accomplishments. This is the evolution of creation. We are here to put our energy into how we evolve on this planet and in this Universe. We are all inextricably linked on a non- physical plane.

And isn't it fun to create? Isn't it fun to invent your own world? I have had a blast writing this book, connecting with the Universe in new and surprising ways, and I hope I meet you on the street one day so that we can meet in physical form. I will thank you from the deep, full, abundant gratitude of my entire being. Why? Because you have allowed me to live my dreams. Thank you. Thank you. Thank you!

Never forget your power! You are as powerful as the divine force that creates the world.

My greatest wish would be for you to use yourself to your fullest potential to create and jump into a world that makes you wake up smiling every day—a really big, dimply smile. That's what your here to do. So what are you going do?

Start creating that world!

Here's to you!

Thank you to the moon and back a million times.

Rich Blessings,

Jen MacFarlane

ACKNOWLEDGMENTS: I want to thank my Beautiful family for supporting me on this journey of taking on my own dreams. My wonderful Husband Craig for feeding me and taking such amazing care of our Son and I as I spent many nights awake working on this book. My Love, Noah for teaching me so many lessons as we grow together. My Mother who loves me like an angel and always encourages me and helps me get through my own roadblocks. My editors, David Steele and Nancy Hartwell who have turned my words into a masterpiece. My friends who sit in deep conversations for hours on end with me; giving me unlimited inspiration. To all of you who have taught me along the way. And to you, the reader, "Thank You" for reading!

WHAT'S NEXT?

If you would like to talk privately, I would love to assist you in your transformational process. We can connect further and work one on one together if you would like. Please contact me here: http://www.astralily.com

My Astralily USchool Training opens twice per year. You can easily stay connected by my private facebook group AstraLily Unleash your Brilliance.

I LOVE YOU! XOXOX

Made in the USA
Charleston, SC
17 March 2015